# DESIGNL_

# TRAINING TO

# SHORTEN TIME

# TO PROFICIENCY

## ONLINE, CLASSROOM AND
## ON-THE-JOB LEARNING STRATEGIES
## FROM RESEARCH

## Dr. Raman K. Attri

Speed To Proficiency Research: S2Pro© Publications

Singapore

ISBN: 978-981-14-0633-1 (e-book)
ISBN: 978-981-14-0632-4 (paperback)
ISBN: 978-981-14-0645-4 (hardcover)

First published: 2019
Lead author: Raman K. Attri
Published by Speed To Proficiency Research: S2Pro©
Published at Singapore
Printed in the United States of America

*National Library Board, Singapore Cataloguing in Publication Data*

Names: Attri, Raman K., 1973-
Title: Designing training to shorten time to proficiency : online, classroom and on-the-job learning strategies from research / Dr Raman K. Attri.
Description: Singapore : Speed To Proficiency Research, 2019 | Includes bibliographic references and index.
Identifiers: OCN 1085692434 | ISBN 978-981-14-0632-4 (paperback) |
    ISBN 978-981-14-0645-4 (hardcover) | ISBN 978-981-14-0633-1 (e-book)
Subject(s): LCSH: Core competencies. | Executive ability.
Classification: DDC 658.4--dc23

**Speed To Proficiency Research: S2Pro©**
*A research and consulting forum*
Singapore 560463
https://www.speedtoproficiency.com
rkattri@speedtoproficiency.com

To Rayan

*21 must-know revelations from a large-scale research study on the classroom, online and on-the-job learning for training leaders of today's business world*

# PREFACE

American scientist Edward Felten once said, "Innovation happens because there are people out there doing and trying a lot of different things." I think that any innovation comes with skills possessed by people in the organizations. Without the well-equipped and skilled workforce, no company can dream of any innovation. It is crucial for the sustainable existence of any company to develop their employees' knowledge, skills, and performance to the desired level. The business is not only changing at a high pace, but it is also becoming overly complex. The skills and knowledge acquired today become irrelevant or obsolete as early as tomorrow. In that kind of dynamics, it is indeed not viable for businesses to wait for months and years for their employees to become proficient in the critical skills required to support the business, customers, and competition.

During my 25 years of professional career in solving complex organizational problems, I have seen the need for "speeding" up the "time" as a universal need across all businesses. The speed with which innovations and technologies are changing our lives is incredible. By the time we adopt one technology, the next generation of the same technology is already knocking at the door. While serving as Senior Global Technical Training Manager at a 15-billion dollar semiconductor corporation, I saw that merely one day of delay in launching a product could cost a company millions of dollars. This business reality of cut-throat competition between global organizations is inevitable.

Now, part of that challenge is that organizations have been struggling to bring their employees up to speed on job-related skills and waiting for years for them to come up to the desired level of performance. Though they understand they must compress time to proficiency of employees, it appears that the training experts in most of the organizations are not able to put an effective or result-giving mechanism in place to accelerate the proficiency of employees. The biggest reason probably is the lack of proven knowledge-base to use, test and develop upon. In my humble opinion, this lack arises due to a weak linkage between practice and research.

In today's business world, we see two set of training and learning leaders out there. The first category of leaders is who apparently do not have an answer (or do not have access to the right answer) how they go about equipping their employees with the required skills at a faster pace. The past learning research on such critical business issues does not make it to the desk of a training manager, who is likely not accustomed to reading through vast academic research literature out there. So even if some answers in some shape and form exist in previous research studies, managers do not generally get access to that knowledge easily and never get to apply it.

On the other hand, there is this second category of training leaders or experts who are well-connected to past scholarly research and able to apply some of those best practices in their contexts and see what works. Some of them seem to have found the answer to 'speed of performance' through experimentation or project work. However, they face different types of constraints altogether which inhibit their findings going out of their walls. As business managers and training leaders, they are not allowed to publish (non-disclosure clauses, intellectual property, trade secrets, etc.). In fact, publishing anyhow is not part of their primary job responsibility or business goal. Generally speaking, they are also not trained to be researchers who could spend thousands of hours to conduct systematic research and produce research papers through the gruesome process of publishing with scholarly journals. Thus, these critical pieces of business know-how they generated during experimentations at organizations or during their primary job gets lost due to the logistics of all this.

It is reasonable to say that the linkage between learning research and the practitioners' world is missing from two sides. First is the lack of transfer of knowledge about practically viable strategies from academic researchers back to the business leaders to try them out. Second is the lack of transfer of information about practical, proven strategies observed by business leaders back into academic researchers' hand to validate and disseminate widely. So as researchers, we do not know for sure what works in reality and what not, though there could be some theoretical and empirical evidence. That is probably the biggest reason why over 50 years of training and development research appears to have not been successful as yet to equip most organizations in getting a good handle on developing their employees up to the desired performance at a "speed" and find the answers to this problem of 'speed to proficiency.'

I undertook this challenge during my doctorate research program at Southern Cross University Australia and conducted a massive practice-oriented, business-focused research to explore the business strategies (methods, techniques, processes, models) that have given proven results in successfully reducing time to proficiency in the organizations. This massive study included over 85 global experts from 7 countries who brought a range of successful strategies to shorten time to proficiency of their employees, shared their success stories via 66 start-to-end project cases and contributed their experience from over 50 different organizations. As I engaged further in in-depth conversations with these thought leaders, business leaders and professionals around the globe, several patterns of initial findings started emerging. Though the goal of the research study was to explore business-level strategies (training and non-training), the initial patterns on training strategies, curriculum design and instructional methods caught my attention. As a global training specialist, I was anxious to see and to validate my past experience in regards to what training and learning strategies were used by leading business leaders to shorten time to proficiency of their employees successfully. These initial findings were presented at some leading international conferences on training, learning, and education. This book has emerged out of the preliminary findings presented in those conferences.

In a conversation, Dr. Charles Jennings, a renowned business leader, mentioned that 'formal training is just 10% of the overall equation.' Exactly on those lines, my research study led to developing an overarching 'model of accelerated proficiency' in which training-related strategies formed a 'small' part of the process of accelerating proficiency of employees. Though training was a small part of the overall equation of accelerated proficiency, it had an indisputable role in developing the skills and performance of people, especially in new roles or new jobs. This book focuses on how training and learning strategies should be structured or implemented to contribute significantly toward shortening time to proficiency of employees. This book is written for business practitioners, training managers, training leaders, learning specialists and instructional designers to apply and test the methods/strategies mentioned in this book to build training programs that can potentially shorten time to proficiency of employees at the workplace.

Though small, this book adds an intriguing contribution to the existing knowledge base in the field of training, learning, instructional design, performance, and expertise. This book is an attempt to bring a 'real' business problem which has a tremendous impact on the bottom-line of the organizations. As researchers, when we realize there is a problem worth solving, we set to find the answers. Through this book, I encourage other researchers to investigate the strategies, methods, and approaches to accelerate time to proficiency of employees in a business context.

Raman K. Attri
January 2019

*'The empirical fact about expertise (i.e., that it takes a long time) sets the stage for an effort at demonstrating the acceleration of the achievement of proficiency.'*

*(Hoffman, Andrews & Feltovich 2012, p. 9)*

# CONTENTS

## CHAPTER 7

## CHAPTER 8

## CHAPTER 9

# ABOUT THE BOOK

This book deals with solving a pressing organizational challenge of bringing employees up to speed faster. In the fast-paced business world, organizations need faster readiness of employees to handle the complex responsibilities of their jobs. The author conducted an extensive doctoral research study with 85 global experts across 66 project cases to explore the practices and strategies that were proven to reduce time to proficiency of employees in a range of organizations worldwide.

This book provides the readers with a first-hand account of findings exclusively related to training and learning strategies, instructional methods, and curriculum design. This book delivers over 21 training and learning strategies across online learning, classroom instructions, and on-the-job learning. These strategies will allow training designers and learning specialists to design workplace training programs that hold the potential to shorten time to proficiency of employees.

The book not only describes findings of the study and theoretical underpinnings, but it also provides practical guidance for implementation to equip corporate learning specialists, HR professionals, training leaders, performance consultants, and direct managers.

Chapter 1 of the book introduces the research study that was conducted and describes the sampling, participants, data collection and data analysis methodology.

Chapter 2 introduces the concept and definition of accelerated proficiency and metrics such as time to proficiency and speed to proficiency. The chapter sets the premise for the business need that demands learning designers to explore methods to shorten time to proficiency of employees.

Chapter 3 describes the result of proficiency curve analysis that revealed four possible trajectories to accelerate employee proficiency.

Chapter 4 introduces the four key hurdles in the form of the inefficiencies of traditional training models that hamper the acceleration of proficiency. This chapter sets the stage what needs to be avoided when designing training meant to accelerate proficiency.

Chapter 5 addresses the group of findings related to online or e-learning. A conceptual model is presented to describe five e-learning strategies with the great potential to accelerate proficiency in workplace skills.

Chapter 6 focuses on findings grouped as the formal classroom or instructor-led instructional strategies. The chapter specifies five instructional strategies to design classroom training and deliver an enriched learning experience to put learners on an accelerated proficiency path.

Chapter 7 explains the findings grouped as on-the-job learning or workplace learning strategies. The chapter describes three strategies for workplace learning design to leverage workplace opportunities and interventions which reported great potential to accelerate proficiency. The chapter presents a conceptual model of workplace learning strategies to guide the implementation of these strategies.

Chapter 8 consolidate the strategies for online learning, classroom learning and workplace learning into a simple model for training design that holds the potential to create training that can contribute into shortening time to proficiency of the employees.

Chapter 9 concludes the book with final thoughts on the role of training and learning strategies toward accelerating proficiency in the long run.

# ABOUT THE AUTHOR

Raman K Attri is a corporate business researcher, learning strategist, and management consultant with a strong zeal to enable people to unravel human learning and performance. He specializes in providing the competitive and strategic value to the organizations by accelerating time-to-proficiency of employees through well-researched models. He holds a doctorate in business from Southern Cross University, Australia. His international professional career spanned over 25 years across a range of disciplines such as scientific research, systems engineering, management consulting, training operations, professional teaching, and learning design. A strong proponent of learning as the core of human success, he provides advisory on accelerated learning techniques which earned him over 60 educational credentials including doctorate degrees, three masters' degrees and tens of international certifications. Despite physical disability since childhood, he leveraged it to learn, research and test a range of "how to methods" to accelerate the rate of personal learning and professional performance at the workplace. He has published his methods in scholarly journals, blogs, books, and conferences. He also runs a non-profit consulting forum focused on researching strategies to accelerate speed to proficiency.

# ABBREVIATIONS

| | |
|---|---|
| ALA | Action Learning Activities |
| CTS | Critical-to-success |
| EPSS | Electronic performance support systems |
| HPT | Human Performance Technology |
| HRD | Human resource development |
| ILT | Instructor-led training |
| JIT | Just-in-time |
| LMS | Learning Management System |
| OJT | On-the-job training |
| PSS | Performance Support Systems |
| ROI | Return on Investment |
| TTP | Time to Proficiency |

# CHAPTER 1

# RESEARCH STUDY: STRATEGIES TO ACCELERATE TIME TO PROFICIENCY

This book is based on the findings of an intensive 5-years long study conducted by the author as part of the doctoral program between the year 2014 to 2018. The research study addressed a much larger question on business practices and strategies to accelerate time to proficiency in organizational settings (Attri 2018). The study is referred to as "*the TTP study*" (time to proficiency study) henceforth.

## 1.1    THE RESEARCH STUDY

### Research background

Past research studies on workplace training and learning suggested that there was a range of training and learning strategies to enhance training outcomes and make learning more effective, including enhancing training transfer to the workplace. Some of those research studies also provide strategies to accelerate skill acquisition. However, there is a very limited amount of research efforts to develop a holistic framework to guide the design and delivery of training at the workplace with a goal to reduce time to proficiency in business organizations. The fair but pressing question that emerges is: How can time to proficiency of the workforce be shortened? What are the strategies or practices that work? How should training and learning be structured to hasten the path to proficiency? This gap was the central area of focus of the research study titled *"Modelling Accelerated Proficiency in Organisations: Practices and Strategies to Shorten Time-to-Proficiency of the Workforce"* conducted by the author at Southern Cross Univerity (Attri 2018).

*The TTP study* addressed a critical challenge in modern organizations: the workforce generally takes a significant amount of time to reach full proficiency in several job roles, which in turn puts the market and financial pressures on organizations. This study aimed to explore practices and strategies that have successfully reduced time to proficiency of the workforce in large multinational organizations, and develop a model based on them.

This study takes forward the conceptualization of *accelerated proficiency* and *accelerated expertise* proposed in experimental research studies conducted by Hoffman (Hoffman et al. 2008, 2009, 2014; Hoffman, Andrews & Feltovich 2012; Hoffman & Andrews 2012; Hoffman, Andrews, et al. 2010; Hoffman, Feltovich, et al. 2010) and Fadde (Fadde & Klein 2010, 2012; Fadde 2007, 2009a, 2009b, 2009c, 2012, 2013, 2016) during the last decade in training and work settings. In their studies, they have identified several theoretical issues and gaps. In particular, gaps such as lack of a good understanding of the concept and process of accelerated proficiency the needs for accelerating proficiency and methods to accelerate the proficiency served to propose research questions in this research study toward accelerating proficiency in the organizational and workplace domain.

**Research questions**

The central research question of this study was: How can organizations accelerate time to proficiency of employees in the workplace? *The TTP study* addressed three aspects: the meaning of accelerated proficiency, as seen by business leaders; the business factors driving the need for a shorter time to proficiency and benefits accrued from it; and practices and strategies to shorten time to proficiency of the workforce.

## 1.2    RESEARCH METHODOLOGY

**Approach**

The business problem of accelerating proficiency is relatively new, and it needs to be understood in its natural settings. Additionally, mechanisms and strategies to accelerate proficiency of the workforce may vary from one organization to another and may even vary among different jobs within the same organization, making it a highly contextual complex phenomenon. It was important to know why some strategies worked in one context and not in others. Therefore, an exploratory qualitative research approach was used to understand '*how things work in particular contexts*' (Mason 2002).

The principal research question was to explore the strategies in terms of "what works" and has been proven to work successfully concerning shortening time to proficiency.

## Participants

*The TTP study* design involved purposive sampling and criteria-driven sampling because only a limited number of experts were expected to possess "know-how" in the area of accelerated proficiency. Professional databases (e.g., social media, ASTD, ISPI, LinkedIn and other conference references) were used to find the potential experts suiting the research goals. The most important criteria for the recruitment of the participants in this study was that participant must have specific experience in reducing time to proficiency of the workforce in organizations.

A systematic criterion was applied to validate the relevant experience of the potential participants. This included evidence of leading at least one project related to accelerated proficiency or time to proficiency, explicitly in written media (e.g., industry reports, interviews, company newsletters, conference presentations, webinars, books, journal or magazine article authorship, white papers, blog posts, etc.); recognitions earned (e.g., industry awards, nominations, etc.) or association/ affiliation with a society, forum, client, company or organization whose charter related to accelerated proficiency; employment or association with the organizations or companies known to have run projects specific to accelerated time to proficiency; self-acclaimed experience on a project or consulting achievement related to accelerated proficiency or time to proficiency in the media (e.g., a LinkedIn resume, internet profiles, academic CVs, responses to research questionnaires, personal communication, etc.).

Among the 371 potential participants identified using the above criteria, 85 project leaders and business leaders finally participated in the study. These participants consisted of global training experts and business professionals with proven project experience in shortening time to proficiency of employees, in various capacities such as project leader, project owner, project designer or project team member (henceforth collectively termed as 'project leaders'). The participants hailed from 7 different countries, with 77% of the participants from the

USA. The participants belonged to 24 different industries, with the majority of the participants being CEOs, consultants, or an equivalent. The mean number of years of experience was more than 20 years, and the majority of the participants had more than 11 years of experience. Most of the project leaders were highly educated, with 35% holding doctoral degrees and 39% holding master's degrees. The distribution profile of the participants is shown in table 1.

*Table 1: The distribution profile of the study participants*

| Participant's country | | | |
|---|---|---|---|
| USA | | 66 | 77% |
| Australia | | 5 | 6% |
| Netherlands | | 5 | 6% |
| UK | | 4 | 5% |
| Singapore | | 3 | 4% |
| UAE | | 1 | 1% |
| Philippines | | 1 | 1% |
| | Total | 85 | 100% |

| Participant's current industry | | | |
|---|---|---|---|
| Professional training & coaching | | 18 | 20% |
| Management consulting | | 13 | 15% |
| Education management | | 7 | 8% |
| Computer software | | 6 | 7% |
| Higher education | | 6 | 7% |
| Semiconductors | | 6 | 7% |
| Research | | 5 | 6% |
| E-learning | | 5 | 6% |
| Information technology & services | | 3 | 4% |
| Oil & energy | | 2 | 2% |
| Financial services | | 2 | 2% |
| Oil & energy | | 1 | 1% |
| Military | | 1 | 1% |
| Broadcast media | | 1 | 1% |
| Public relations & communications | | 1 | 1% |
| Electrical/Electronic manufacturing | | 1 | 1% |
| Education technology | | 1 | 1% |
| Banking | | 1 | 1% |
| Management consulting | | 1 | 1% |
| Internet | | 1 | 1% |
| Human resources | | 1 | 1% |
| Information services | | 1 | 1% |
| Unknown | | 1 | 1% |
| | Total | 85 | 100% |

5

| Participant's current position/title | | | |
|---|---|---|---|
| President/CEO/MD/Founder | | 27 | 32% |
| Researcher/Scientist/Academician/Author | | 13 | 15% |
| Consultant | | 12 | 13% |
| Program/Training manager | | 10 | 12% |
| Director/VP | | 9 | 11% |
| Trainer/Facilitator / Instructional designer | | 6 | 7% |
| CLO/CKO | | 5 | 6% |
| Leadership/HRD specialist | | 2 | 2% |
| Retired | | 1 | 1% |
| | **Total** | **85** | **100%** |

| Participant's education | | | |
|---|---|---|---|
| Doctorate | | 29 | 35% |
| Masters | | 34 | 39% |
| Bachelors | | 16 | 19% |
| No information | | 6 | 7% |
| | **Total** | **85** | **100%** |

| Participant's experience range (in years) | | | |
|---|---|---|---|
| 0 to 10 | | 3 | 4% |
| 11 to 20 | | 24 | 27% |
| 21 to 30 | | 22 | 26% |
| 31 to 40 | | 24 | 29% |
| 41 to 50 | | 7 | 8% |
| Unknown | | 5 | 6% |
| | **Total** | **85** | **100%** |

## Sampling unit

The "what works" philosophy also guided this research study to use *bounded project cases* as a sampling unit. Bounded project case is a case (i.e., a success story of a phenomenon in a bounded context) which has a defined start and end (i.e., a project), and it is bounded (i.e., its boundaries are defined in terms of scope) (Merriam & Tisdell 2016; Miles, Huberman & Saldana 2014; Turner & Müller 2003). The goal of the data collection was to gather and understand successful project cases (what worked). This would provide insights into the need for shortening time to proficiency. It would also reveal strategies employed by business leaders in achieving it, as well as indicate results attained out of deploying such strategies. This sampling unit specified a constraint that the participant must be a project leader, project owner, project designer or some senior project team member who had the rich and first-hand details of all aspects of the project.

A total of 66 successful project cases, along with 50 associated project case documents were collected. The collected project cases were categorized in four broad categories of contextual variables (1) Sectors: Economic, business or industry; (2) Nature of the job role; (3) Critical-to-success (CTS) skills: primary skills for the job; and (4) Complexity levels: the complexity of the skill or the job role or both. These project cases spanned across 10 economic sectors, 21 business sectors, and 30 industry groups, covering 15 different types of jobs, 16 different critical-to-success skills involved in those jobs and 5 levels of complexity, as shown in table 2.

*Table 2: The distribution profile of project cases analyzed in the study*

| Business sector classification of the project case (Thomas-Reuters Business Classification system) | | |
|---|---|---|
| Technology Equipment | 12 | 18% |
| Energy - Fossil Fuels | 8 | 12% |
| Banking & Investment Services | 6 | 9% |
| Pharmaceuticals & Medical Research | 4 | 6% |
| Healthcare Services | 4 | 6% |
| Software & IT Services | 3 | 5% |
| Government / Military | 3 | 5% |
| Industrial & Commercial Services | 3 | 5% |
| Industrial Goods | 3 | 5% |
| Insurance | 3 | 5% |
| Automobiles & Auto Parts | 2 | 3% |
| Telecommunications Services | 2 | 3% |
| Cyclical Consumer Services | 2 | 3% |
| Mineral Resources | 2 | 3% |
| Retailers | 2 | 3% |
| Food & Beverages | 2 | 3% |
| Transportation | 1 | 2% |
| Sports | 1 | 2% |
| Utilities | 1 | 2% |
| Chemicals | 1 | 2% |
| Real Estate | 1 | 2% |
| **Total** | **66** | 100% |

| The primary job role of employees | | |
|---|---|---|
| Technical or Engineering | 22 | 33% |
| Sales - Non-Technical | 9 | 14% |
| Scientific or Development | 6 | 9% |
| Strategic Management, Leadership | 4 | 6% |
| Managerial, Supervisory | 4 | 6% |
| Customer service helpdesk | 4 | 6% |
| Production, Manufacturing | 3 | 5% |
| Medical, Healthcare | 3 | 5% |
| Sales - Technical | 3 | 5% |
| Financial services | 2 | 3% |
| Training or Education | 2 | 3% |
| Warehouse | 1 | 2% |
| Sports, Athletics | 1 | 2% |
| Management consulting | 1 | 2% |
| Assembly, Repair | 1 | 2% |
| Total | 66 | 100% |

| Critical-to-success skills in the sampled job | | |
|---|---|---|
| Sales and negotiation | 12 | 18% |
| Complex troubleshooting | 12 | 18% |
| Technical Problem solving | 7 | 11% |
| Innovation and design | 6 | 9% |
| Strategic thinking | 4 | 6% |
| Supervisory | 4 | 6% |
| Helpdesk support | 4 | 6% |
| Project execution | 3 | 5% |
| Precision machining | 3 | 5% |
| Medical and psychological care | 3 | 5% |
| Financial analysis | 2 | 3% |
| Teaching and training | 2 | 3% |
| Perceptual and physical skills | 1 | 2% |
| Data processing | 1 | 2% |
| Business analysis | 1 | 2% |
| Assembly | 1 | 2% |
| Total | 66 | 100% |

| Location of the project case | | |
|---|---|---|
| USA | 55 | 83% |
| Netherlands | 3 | 5% |
| Singapore | 3 | 5% |
| Australia | 2 | 3% |
| UK | 1 | 2% |
| Philipines | 1 | 2% |
| UAE | 1 | 2% |
| Total | 66 | 100% |

## Data collection and interviews

Each project leader that consented to participate in the study was asked to provide one project case in detail. Accordingly, interviews were structured around five core elements which essentially described a story in a project as follows: (1) business challenge or problem of time to proficiency to be solved; (2) description of the previous solution in place (if any) to reduce time to proficiency and previous results (business metrics); (3) issues or challenges with the previous solution and root cause of the problem; (4) description of the new solutions or strategies implemented to reduce time to proficiency; and (5) the results in terms of reduction in time to proficiency (quantitative, qualitative or anecdotal results).

Three types of interviews were incorporated into the research design, in order to collect data from the project leaders: (1) in-depth qualitative interviews; (2) questionnaire interviews; and (3) e-mail interviews. The primary method used for data collection was in-depth interviews, to understand this new phenomenon in rich detail. These interviews, structured around bounded project case descriptions, allowed consistent data, and hence added to the data quality and completeness. Furthermore, this approach allowed easy cross-case analysis by comparing the bounded projects cases across several variables in order to understand commonality, differences, transferability and generalizability (Bower et al. 2015; Miles, Huberman & Saldana 2014; Stake 2006; Vohra 2014; Yin 2014).

## Data analysis

The data analysis used two rigorous methodologies in juxtaposition - thematic analysis techniques specified by Boyatzis (1998) and Braun & Clarke (2006, 2013), and matrix analysis approach specified by Miles & Huberman (1994) and Miles, Huberman & Saldana (2014).

9

Using thematic analysis techniques specified by Boyatzis (1998) and Braun & Clarke (2006, 2013), new themes and patterns were identified, and emergent data-driven coding was used to code these themes and patterns. The themes were analyzed for the association, relationship, and hierarchy among themes. The themes, sub-themes and overarching themes emerged during thematic analysis.

The themes were then arranged in the form of matrices using the matrix analysis framework specified by Miles, Huberman & Saldana (2014). Each matrix was basically a table of columns and rows to arrange the data for easy viewing in one place. The matrix analysis approach arranges themes and data of bounded project cases in the form of a matrix to understand the dynamics of the project cases within itself and then across the project cases by stacking rows of data from other project cases.

These matrices were used to compare the themes across the several variables in all the project cases (Stake 2006; Yin 2014). Project cases were compared for similarity, patterns, and contrast; and the relationship of those patterns across different contextual variables such as business sectors, industry groups, nature of jobs, nature of skills involved and complexity ratings was determined.

First, the within-case analysis was performed, in which one row of a given project case was read all the way across to all the columns. This enabled a thorough understanding of the dynamics of a project case, based on various characteristics, variables, and contexts, as well as understanding the full start-to-end project success story. The full picture included a snapshot of business challenges; inefficiencies of previous models; factors and determinants; philosophical stands; proficiency measures; inputs; processes, methods, techniques, and practices used in each of the projects; and the project results. This analysis of projects was first focused on one project in its entirety. Then the researcher moved on to next project case that revealed certain new insights with which he went back and reviewed the previously analyzed case or cases to redefine, or redraft, or change something in the light of new learning.

Then, the cross-case analysis was conducted for project cases collected across different contexts such as different organizations, industries, business environment, job types, complexity levels, and countries. Comparison of themes among different contexts was made. In the cross-case analysis, each variable or each theme was picked one-at-a-time and then read vertically along that column through all the project cases. Variations of key themes from one project case to another were noted. The themes were validated by a constant comparison of themes with each other across all the project cases. Some themes were refined or collapsed or expanded, while some were merged. Several display forms were constructed before reaching a useful view, which enabled the drawing of meaningful conclusions.

Then the projects were grouped by contextual variables such as the economic sector, business sector, generic job role, nature of primary skill and complexity level. The sub-matrices were used to analyze the patterns of the themes across these contextual variables to see the association and relationships. This was an iterative process, going back-and-forth between data, codes, themes, concept maps, and matrices. This rigorous recursive processes of completing data reduction, creating data display and drawing conclusions led to the development of a conceptual model of accelerated proficiency based on six major practices, and twenty-four strategies which prevailed across all project cases.

## Expert focus group validation

Ten project leaders were invited from different backgrounds and industries to participate in an expert focus group review. The purpose of this focus group of experts was to review the findings of the research study and conceptual model developed during data analysis and sought feedback on validity, transferability, and utilization of the findings. The experts were selected based on their demonstrated leadership, diversity of business sectors, and the probability of receiving responses.

The model and findings were presented to the focus group as a thirty-page document using one round of 'feed-forward' Delphi method to elicit inputs from these experts, by 'presenting to respondents the information about emerging consensus derived from the prior interviews' (Gordon 1994, p. 5). The experts were asked some specific questions and allowed to provide their comments. Their feedback was used to validate the model and findings, and the necessary refinement was done in the analysis.

**Generalizability and transferability**

Framework and techniques specified by Lincoln & Guba (1985) and Miles, Huberman & Saldana (2014) were used to ensure objectivity, dependability, and credibility of the study data, data analysis, and findings.

The sampling of 85 project leaders used in the study was much larger compared to any standards specified for a qualitative study. The project cases spanned across over 50 different organizational settings and were not contained in a specific industry or business.

Additionally, data triangulation was used by gathering in-depth interviews as well as evidence from documentation gathered from various sources like write-ups, case studies, presentations, blog posts, white papers, and magazine articles related to the project case under discussion. Further, multiple supplementary techniques were utilized. The techniques included matrix analysis, thematic analysis, concept maps, thematic maps, thematic networks, template analysis, within-case, and cross-case comparative analysis. All of these techniques collectively enhanced the data analysis and improved the representation of participants' experience.

A prevalence analysis was conducted to test for generalizability and transferability. This analysis verified that each theme and each strategy included in the final model were indeed strongly prevalent across the majority of the project cases. This analysis was further strengthened by peer review from highly experienced professionals as well as a thorough review of findings with experts in the focus group.

As a result of the application of rigorous reliability and validation best practices, the findings of this study were found exhibiting a high level of generalizability, transferability, applicability, and fittingness across a broader range of contexts. Collectively, the model generated in this study was found to be generalizable across several contexts.

## 1.3    RESEARCH OUTCOMES

The research study revealed six overarching business practices employed by organizations to reduce time to proficiency. Organizations orchestrated these six business practices as an input-output-feedback system to reduce time to proficiency of the workforce. A conceptual model titled *Accelerated Proficiency Model* was developed representing interactions among six business-level practices/processes as a closed-loop system to explain the concept and process of accelerated proficiency in the workplace. These practices were implemented through a set of twenty-four strategies proven successful in various contexts. A two-level hierarchical framework titled *6/24 framework of strategies* was also constructed in the form of a checklist consisting of six practices and twenty-four strategies for practitioners. Overall, the findings of this research study contribute significantly to the body of knowledge on accelerated proficiency.

As a preamble to the remaining book, it must be noted that *the TTP study* was focused primarily on overall business practices/ strategies and was not limited to a given academic discipline. The final model that evolved at the final stages was the overarching model spanning much beyond training and learning domains and includes strategies at management and job-level.

## 1.4   TRAINING AND LEARNING STRATEGIES

While the overall investigation was conducted to explore business practices/strategies, *the TTP study* did lead to several early findings on training and learning strategies which were seen to help accelerate time to proficiency of the workforce. This section of the findings in the research study specifically answer the question: *What and how training experts use specific training strategies (methods, techniques, mechanisms, systems, processes, instructional design, methodologies, interventions, etc.) in various contexts in leading organizations which have successfully reduced time to proficiency of employees in complex job skills?*

The findings from this research question revealed approaches and strategies which were grounded in training and learning efforts. These strategies were then categorized into three categories based on the nature of training and learning strategies:

- E-learning design strategies
- Classroom instructor-led instructional strategies
- Workplace learning strategies

At a high level, these strategies suggested what needs to happen from a training and learning design standpoint, if organizations strive to shorten time to proficiency of employees. These early results were presented in leading international conferences and published in the conference proceedings.

This book presents the important observations noticed from preliminary findings that focused on developing and accelerating employee learning, skills, and performance. Various aspects of employee development are discussed in this book which includes training and learning, skill acquisition, instructional methods, curriculum, and training design.

## 1.5   HOW THE BOOK IS ORGANIZED

Chapter 2 provides the foundational understanding of various definitions of terms like time to proficiency, time to competence, time to full productivity, speed to proficiency and relate it to the concept of acceleration. The chapter provides an introduction to the importance of shortening time to proficiency as a business need in organizations.

Chapter 3 described an overall analysis of the proficiency curve which leads to the identification of four different approaches to accelerating time to proficiency in the workplace. This chapter acts as a conceptual backbone to the remainder of the book by highlighting four phases of the training cycle.

Chapter 4 introduces the findings on the inefficiencies of traditional training models that hamper the acceleration of proficiency. This chapter describes four major inefficiencies in traditional training models and sets the stage for what needs to be avoided when designing training meant to accelerate proficiency.

Chapter 5 explain the five strategies for designing e-learning that can support faster initial readiness of employees, which goes a long way toward shortening time to proficiency.

Chapter 6 describes the strategies related to improving classroom or instructor-led training sessions which are an inseparable part of most organizational training endeavors. The chapter specifies five instructional strategies that can accelerate the proficiency of learners.

Chapter 7 details three unique strategies that emerged from the research study that specifies how learning designers can leverage the work assignments and activities to truly transform the training focused on shortening time to proficiency on the job.

Chapter 8 consolidate the strategies for online learning, classroom learning and workplace learning into a simple model for training design that holds the potential to create training that can contribute into shortening time to proficiency of the employees.

Chapter 9 concludes the book with a bigger picture that establishes that accelerating time to proficiency requires a total eco-system much beyond the training interventions. The chapter summarizes the underlying value of training, though it is a small part of the overall efforts and endeavors required to accelerate the proficiency of the workforce.

# CHAPTER 2

# IMPORTANCE OF SHORTENING EMPLOYEES' TIME TO PROFICIENCY

Lately, the term *speed to proficiency* has taken its own little life in the business world. Terms like *time to proficiency* and *speed to proficiency* are increasingly becoming metrics in the new business world. However, in *the TTP study*, business leaders expressed how poorly the term "speed to proficiency" and for that sake "accelerating time to proficiency" is understood by their frontline managers (Attri 2018). They also indicated the concerns of how academic community and scholarly literature view these terms differently. Scholarly literature tends to express several different meanings of term speed to proficiency. This chapter summarizes some key definitions and outlines a few implications of these terms.

## 2.1   PROFICIENCY OR PROFICIENT WORKFORCE

Business articles and academic papers continue to emphasize the composition of proficiency in terms of knowledge, skills, and competencies to perform the desired function. For example, Dixon (2015), in her article provided a more straightforward view: 'Proficiency is the quality of having great facility and competence. Every job requires that employees demonstrate certain job competencies to a certain level of proficiency. The competencies are 'a set of observable behaviors that provide a structured guide to help identify, evaluate and develop key knowledge, skills, and attitudes to perform the job effectively' [https://talentculture.com/time-to-proficiency-orientation-and-onboarding/].

A highly regarded business leader, Fred Charles, considered to be the first one to coin and define the term "speed to proficiency" as:

> Proficiency is the use of knowledge in action for the purpose of producing value for a customer. The proficiency threshold, therefore, is the exact moment when a worker can convert knowledge through action into the promised value for the customer. (Fred 2002, p. 43)

He further qualified it by saying:

> The proficiency threshold is reached when sales and marketing team can sell and advertise value to customers with confidence, when orders are filled on time, when services meet customer expectations, and when management team is leading as envisioned. (Fred 2002, p. 44)

As we can see, he specified proficiency in terms of business metrics about which an organization would care.

Leading thought leaders on *Learning Paths* defined proficiency as: 'Being able to perform a given task or function up to a predetermined standard. Proficiency and independently productive are often used as synonyms' (Rosenbaum & Williams 2004, p. 5). They further iterated: 'This is the point in time when you are left totally on your own and that *[sic]* you can do your job without asking questions or making mistakes' (Rosenbaum & Williams 2004, p. 13). They also specified consistency as one of the key components of proficiency, that is, achieving performance thresholds once is not proficiency: 'Proficiency is when a new employee achieves a predetermined level of performance on a consistent basis. Proficiency can be defined in number of transactions, dollars sold, defect rates, customer satisfaction scores, or anything else that is measurable and related to results' (Rosenbaum & Williams 2004, p. 14). Their later qualification clearly set it as a business metrics, that is, proficiency needs to be measured in business key performance indicators (KPIs), and metrics associated with a job role.

On the same lines, a white paper from Alorica (2017, p. 7) defines: 'To be truly proficient, an agent must master not only the required skills for the position, but be able to work independently while meeting all KPIs.'

In *the TTP study*, the author found that most of the business leaders thought proficiency in terms on how well someone performs a job or function as opposed to skills/knowledge, which of course are ingredients that form the proficiency but do not reflect the whole. The business leaders emphasized the business metrics as the way to define proficiency. The research analysis identified it as 'job-role proficiency' to differentiate it from definitions of proficiency used in task and skill domains:

> Job-role proficiency is *[sic]* state of performance at which performers produce business outcomes or deliverables consistently to the set performance thresholds expected from a given job role. It refers to achieving and maintaining one pre-established performance level and does not imply progression through different stages or levels of performance.

It refers to the business performance of the job role and does not convey an individual's performance demonstrated on a task or skill' (Attri 2018, p. 236).

This finding substantially differed from the ones presented in academic research which mostly position proficiency in terms of tasks or skills.

## 2.2   DEFINITION OF NEW BUSINESS METRICS

Recent research studies have shown that the business world has reacted to increased competition and pace of business. Thus there is increasing use of new business metrics to track the performance of the workforce. Some most common new metrics tied to 'time' and 'speed' are:

- Time to proficiency
- Speed to proficiency
- Time to competence
- Time to full productivity

**Time To Proficiency**

Among the earliest use of the term "time to proficiency," Carpenter et al. (1989) measured time to proficiency in terms of performance in a selected set of tasks. They defined: 'Time to proficiency as the length of time it takes to bring people with different attributes (especially mental aptitude) to targeted levels of task performance' (Carpenter et al. 1989, p. 1). They correlated productivity, attrition, cost, and aptitude in their model with the time to proficiency.

In the same time frame, Pinder & Schroeder (1987) conducted time to proficiency study which involved 354 managers from eight companies in Canada, who were surveyed regarding their time to proficiency after job transfers. They conceived time to proficiency as 'the length of time that elapses between the individual's movement into a new job and ascendancy of that individual to a level of performance at which a balance between inducements and contributions exists' (Pinder & Schroeder 1987, p. 337). Inducements were the investments made in the person when s/he started a new job, while contributions were his/her productivity on the new job. This definition reveals the key implication that while someone is working toward desired proficiency and trying to be productive in a new job, his or her performance has a financial impact on the business, thus making it a compelling reason to monitor time to proficiency in a given job.

Renowned academic researchers on *accelerated proficiency,* Hoffman et al. (2014, p. 169) referred to time to proficiency in terms of career stages, as the time taken by an individual to reach a desired level of proficiency. The career stages they most frequently referred to were - journeyman and senior journeyman. The journeyman career stage exhibited characteristics like being reliable, experienced, able to work unsupervised, and having achieved a certain level of competence.

However, the concept of time to proficiency is seen differently by business leaders, who take the concept from the task domain or career domain typically mentioned in the most academic research studies to the job domain. For instance, *Training Industry*'s glossary pitches it as: 'Time to proficiency refers to the time needed or taken by an individual to acquire the skills and knowledge necessary to reach an acceptable level of performance' [https://trainingindustry.com/glossary/time-to-proficiency/].

Contemporary business leaders consider it very important to identify the point when an individual demonstrates performance that signifies his/her being operating at or above desired or target proficiency (Fred 2002). Every job role requires a certain amount of time to develop performance to the desired proficiency level. This time is referred to as *time to proficiency* (TTP). Leading *Learning Paths* gurus define it as: 'The time it takes to reach a predetermined level of proficiency. In other words, the time from day one to independently productive' (Rosenbaum & Williams 2004, p. 5). More recently, Bachlechner et al. (2010, p. 378) defined time to proficiency as 'the amount of time an individual spends in a new job environment before it [sic] is able to fulfil most tasks without help from colleagues or supervisors.'

It appears that time to proficiency is not the measurement of one activity; rather it involves time required for several activities such as onboarding, formal as well as informal training required to understand the basics of the job, on-the-job training and on-the-job learning to understand specifics of job tasks, and other activities to gain experience on specific tasks or skills required to do the job (Attri & Wu 2015). Time to proficiency is usually measured from the date of hiring, or when someone takes up a new role or the first day of the training s/he attends. However, measurement of the starting point and end state may vary significantly based on the context and definition of desired proficiency.

**Speed To Proficiency**

The literature review suggested that the earliest usage of the term "speed to proficiency" came from book *Breakaway: Deliver value to your customer – Fast!!!* in which Fred (2002, p. 16) defined:

> Proficient workers speed things up: organizational change, operational improvement, problem solving, and delivery of service all happen faster. When you shorten the time it takes for workers to become proficient, the capital and resources required to introduce a new product, maintain operations and infrastructure, and perform a service are also proportionally reduced. I call this *speed to proficiency*.

In the last decade the term 'speed to proficiency' has become a common buzzword. Cedar Interactive (company) positioned it as:

'"Speed to Proficiency" refers to the time required to bring a person up to a proficient level of performance at a job or task' [http://cedarinteractive. com/serv-speedtopro.htm].

Bruck (2007) identified its value as: 'In any business arena where the demonstrated mastery of new knowledge and skills is critical to the success of the business speed to proficiency is the name of the game' [http://www.q2learning.com/docs/WP-S2P.pdf]. Recently, in a white paper, Alorica (2017, p. 7) defines:

> To be truly proficient, an agent must master not only the required skills for the position, but be able to work independently while meeting all KPIs. How long an individual or team takes to reach this level of competence is the speed to proficiency.

## Time to Competence and Time to Full Productivity

Some leaders like to refer to other terms like time to full productivity. Cornerstone (company) places it as 'Time to productivity is a metric that measures how long it takes a new hire to contribute to an organization' [https://www.cornerstoneondemand.com/glossary/time-productivity]. Millington (2018) states:

Time-to-full productivity can mean one of two things. It can refer to the time it takes a new recruit to ably complete every aspect of their job role as measured by their manager. Alternatively, it can refer to the time it takes a recruit to reach an equivalent level of performance as their closest colleagues. Essentially, it means how long it takes a newcomer to be proficient in their job.

In a survey conducted by i4cp (2011) [https://www.i4cp.com/productivity-blog/2011/09/14/why-you-should-measure-time-to-full-productivity], it was observed:

> Time-to-full-productivity is a metric few organizations use, but which many acknowledge they should be tracking. Just 16% of respondents to an i4cp survey stated that they use the time-to-full-productivity metric to a high or very high extent, but 64% say they should be using it to manage talent more effectively.

KPS (company) considered 'Time to competency is defined as the time to achieve the target performance level' [https://www.kpsol.com/speed-to-competency-service-agents-measurement-action/]. Nevertheless, these terms mean essentially the same thing (or similar things) as the time to proficiency.

## 2.3   ACCELERATED PROFICIENCY

The corporations worldwide have started shifting their focus (or started including the focus) on the necessity for acceleration and speed to develop their workforce at a faster rate, increase the rate of skill acquisition and reduce times with which workforce becomes ready to do their jobs. Such an effort is referred to as accelerating proficiency, accelerating speed to proficiency or reducing/shortening time to proficiency, among other variations of these terms.

**Accelerated Proficiency - Accelerating speed to proficiency or Reducing time to proficiency**

In general, both the phrases *accelerating speed to proficiency* and *reducing time to proficiency* means the same thing. Once the desired level of proficiency is defined, the next challenge is to reach that proficiency level in a shorter time. From a practical standpoint, the business challenge is to bring people to a certain level of proficiency so that they can do their job to the desired standards. Lately, there are some conscientious efforts made by some organizations to institute focused projects to accelerate proficiency. Such projects entail the goal to achieve a shorter time to proficiency in a given job role (or in other words accelerate speed to proficiency).

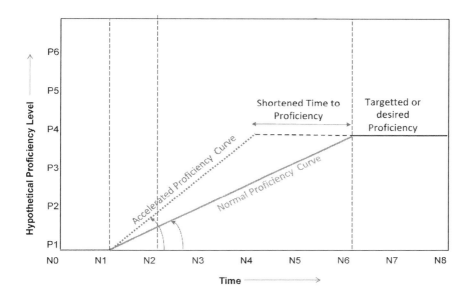

*Figure 1: The concept of accelerating time to proficiency (Copyrights Raman K. Attri)*

In the business and academic literature, this deliberate effort is expressed with several synonyms or variations like accelerating skill acquisition, accelerating proficiency acquisition, accelerating performance, accelerating time to proficiency, shortening time to proficiency and accelerating speed to proficiency (Bruck 2015; Fadde & Klein 2010; Fred 2002; Hoffman et al. 2014; Rosenbaum & Williams 2004). Most commonly, scholarly research calls this concept as 'accelerated proficiency.' The concept of accelerating time to proficiency is depicted in figure 1. This is a simplistic representation in terms of time intervals N0 to N8 on the horizontal axis and hypothetical proficiency P1 to P6 on the vertical axis. The idea is to put focused efforts to allow people to follow *accelerated proficiency curve* (which is a higher rate of proficiency acquisition) as opposed to the *normal proficiency curve* which otherwise people would have followed if nothing was done. By putting together focused efforts the time to reach the desired proficiency P4 in a shorter time N4 compared to previous time N6.

Hoffman, Feltovich, et al. (2010, p. 9) defined *accelerated proficiency* as a 'phenomenon of achieving higher levels of proficiency in less time' (p. 9) and dealt with 'how to train and train quickly to higher levels of proficiency' (p. 8). Hoffman et al. (2014, p. 13) further qualified accelerated proficiency as 'getting individuals to achieve high levels of proficiency at a rate faster than ordinary.'

Their research simplified the definition in terms of career stages too. Hoffman, Andrews & Feltovich (2012, p. 8) considered that accelerated proficiency deals with 'achievement of knowledge and skill across the proficiency spectrum, all the way from apprentice to expert levels' in a shortest possible time. They expressed accelerated proficiency in terms of time to proficiency (p. 169). Thus, accelerated proficiency is the deliberate and conscious effort of shortening time to proficiency. Acceleration of proficiency is measured in terms of reduction in the time someone takes to reach the desired proficiency.

In *the TTP study*, analysis led to identifying core characteristics of the concept of accelerated proficiency:

> *Accelerating proficiency* means shortening the time someone takes in a given job role to reach to a state of consistent performance that meets the set thresholds. This is measured in time-to-proficiency. A clearer definition of job-role proficiency and its measures are the foremost critical requirement to the acceleration of proficiency. Accelerated proficiency is not about learning a body of content faster or shortening the training duration because the solution to a shorter time-to-proficiency lies beyond training interventions (Attri 2018, p. 236).

## The Intent of accelerating proficiency

The question arises if accelerated proficiency is the same or different from the other similar sounding terms like accelerated learning, accelerated training or accelerated expertise.

In *the TTP study*, some key insights revealed that accelerated proficiency (or efforts to reduce time to proficiency) is entirely different from similarly worded topics such as *accelerated learning* and *accelerated training* and *accelerated expertise* (Attri 2018).

Organizations appeared to view accelerated proficiency and accelerated learning to mean two different things. The goal of the traditional meaning of accelerated learning is limited to speeding up the learning curve of a specific individual, that is, learning a given content in a shorter time or learning more content in the same time (e.g. Imel 2002; Patchan et al. 2015; Radler & Bocianu 2017; Trekles & Sims 2013). This intent has a few implications:

Learning something quickly does not necessarily mean an individual would start producing consistent business results quickly too. For example, if a sales engineer's monthly quota were $1M, learning the details of the product features, sales processes and sales technique would not mean s/he could surely produce $1M consistently month after month. S/he would have to develop relationships, connections, and leads, and gain experience in all aspects of the job role to be able to produce that much sales every month. Such outcomes require more than just learning content, knowledge or skills. Thus, the effect of accelerating learning or learning more content in a short time may or may not always contribute toward a shorter time to proficiency.

The reality at the workplace is that people (even in the same job) learn at different rates and with different styles. Controlling every individual's learning curve is not feasible, and that is not the intent of any project involving accelerating proficiency. Accelerated proficiency refers to the performance of a job role as a whole and a group of people serving that role as a whole. Thus, it is not about the learning of one person, unless it is achieved collectively for the entire group in a job (Bologa & Lupu 2007).

Further, the concept of accelerated proficiency is different from the traditional concept of accelerated training or shortening training duration. Accelerated proficiency projects are generally not started with the intent of shortening training duration or rapidized training, that is, 'the idea of training individuals to achieve some minimal level of proficiency at a rate faster than usual' (Hoffman et al. 2014, p. 13). On the contrary, attaining such initial operating readiness to put someone on-the-job to do basic duties does not serve the goal of accelerated proficiency toward reducing time to proficiency. Shortening training duration is not an explicit goal when we focus on accelerating time to proficiency in organizations, though in almost every case, it was attained as a by-product. The true goal of accelerated proficiency (or efforts toward accelerating time to proficiency and accelerating speed to proficiency) is to make someone fully productive and fully functioning on his or her job to produce outcomes designated for the job role.

Additionally, accelerating time to proficiency did not mean to develop the expertise of employees to the highest level at a faster rate. To develop employees to desired proficiency is not the same as developing or accelerating expertise. Expertise is considered to be an elite status bestowed on few domain specialists, and not everyone may need to be developed to that level. At ground level, proficiency and expertise are not the same things. Hoffman, Andrews, and Feltovich (2012, p. 8) expressed their opinion: 'We do not assume that every organization needs to have every employee be expert at every task. Instead, we are recognizing that for the majority of employees achieving a degree of competence to become journeymen is just fine.'

For example, for some critical functions or roles in organizations such as CEO's position, there may be a need to develop individuals to a very high level of proficiency as determined by the nature of the challenges faced. Such brilliant individuals may be experts in their domains. However, not everyone needs to be, or could be an expert of that order.

## 2.4  NEED TO SHORTEN TIME TO PROFICIENCY

The overall time to proficiency could be in months or years depending on the jobs. For example, time to proficiency of new bankers in a study was estimated to be between eleven and fourteen months (Thompson 2017, p. 173). According to an estimate, a pilot takes a minimum of 1500 hours (the equivalent of two years flying two hours every day) to be certified to fly a commercial plane (Government Publishing Office 2013). An air force communication specialist's time to proficiency was noted in the range of 18 months to 36 months depending upon their aptitude scores (Carpenter et al. 1989). In another study involving 300 call center agents, Borton (2007) noted that time to proficiency of the agents was more than six months. More recently, a survey conducted with chief sales officers of 1,200 companies worldwide by Accenture (2013) indicated that time to proficiency of 73% of the new sales representative workforce was approximately one year or more.

Organizations do not have that much time (Fadde & Klein 2010). Market pressure, particularly over the last decade, has warranted accelerating the expertise cycle as a necessity (Clark & Mayer 2013). Wray & Wallace (2011, p. 243) appealed, 'A more realistic aspiration is to create conditions encouraging all individuals to proceed at the maximum pace possible for them, both in training settings and workplace practice.' The result of a shorter time to proficiency leads to substantial financial and operational benefits to the organization and higher value to customers (Fred 2002). Developing employees to the desired level of proficiency is a key goal of organizations for their sustainability (Bruck 2015). 'Proficiency is critical to performance in complex work contexts' (Hoffman, Feltovich, et al. 2010, p. 250).

A decade ago proponents of 10-year of deliberate practice, Ericsson & Charness (1994, p. 737) pointed out that there are no proven ways to develop expertise faster:

> Although these studies [on expertise] have revealed how beginners acquire complex cognitive structures and skills that circumvent the basic limits confronting them, researchers have not uncovered some simple strategies that would allow nonexperts to rapidly acquire expert performance.

Very recently, Hoffman, Andrews & Feltovich (2012, p. 9) raised the issue that 'empirical fact about expertise (i.e., that it takes a long time) sets the stage for an effort at demonstrating the acceleration of the achievement of proficiency.' They further appeal to training professionals:

> Our vision is that methods for accelerating the achievement of proficiency, and even extraordinary expertise, might be taken to new levels such that one can accelerate the achievement of proficiency across the journeyman-to-expert span post-hiring (Hoffman, Andrews & Feltovich 2012, p. 9).

Nevertheless, there is a general consensus that time to achieve a high level of proficiency to do any job consistently and reliably with a high degree of repeatability is generally very long and that sets grounds to put some processes, methodologies, and efforts to build a knowledge-base to reduce it. However, the reality is that even today, there is a lack of proven knowledge-base in the training industry as a whole.

Therefore, business has a pressing need to accelerate speed to proficiency of their employees in almost every job. Fred (2002, p. 16) makes a compelling argument:

Speed to proficiency is more than a theoretical advantage:
It is the most devastating competitive weapon in the world
where the competitive forces of scale, automation, and
capital are subordinate to the power of proficient workforce.

Time is money and any reduction in time should be the first goal
of any training program, while not losing focus on the effectiveness
and quality of the same.

# CHAPTER 3

# FOUR TRAJECTORIES TO ACCELERATE PROFICIENCY[1]

The corporate goal to accelerate proficiency is as intriguing as it is mysterious because there are several possible routes to accelerate proficiency in professional skills. Lajoie (2003), in concept, emphasized that to accelerate the journey from novice to expert, the 'trajectory' to expertise must be established and made clear. Lajoie (2003) proposed understanding what experts know first, gathering explicit exemplars or models of how experts teach novices, responses or examples from experts, and then mapping that to create a trajectory that can help novices to develop similar competencies. She maintained that '[t]he

---

[1] A version of this chapter was presented as a confence paper: Attri, RK 2014, "Rethinking professional skill development in competitive corporate world: accelerating time-to-expertise of employees at workplace," in J Latzo (ed.), *Proceedings of Conference on Education and Human Development in Asia*, Hiroshima, 2-4 March, PRESDA Foundation, Kitanagova, pp. 1–11, http://dx.doi.org/10.13140/RG.2.1.5125.7043.

transition from student to expert professional can be accelerated when a trajectory for change is plotted and made visible to learners' (Lajoie 2003, p. 24). However, there could be multiple trajectories possible depending upon the learners and the goals.

In an attempt to clarify possible trajectories toward accelerating proficiency, a qualitative proficiency curve analysis was conducted by the author (Attri 2014). The analysis was first presented at the conference on Human Development in Asia titled *"Rethinking professional skill development in competitive corporate world: accelerating time-to-expertise of employees at workplace"* (Attri 2014)[2]. The analysis of proficiency curve analysis suggested four conceptual approaches that could potentially accelerate the proficiency acquisition of employees. Simple principles of mathematics such as equations of straight lines, slope, and piece-wise representation were used to derive these trajectories. This chapter describes the basics of four approaches/trajectories which performance specialists could take to accelerate the proficiency of employees.

## 3.1  PROFICIENCY CURVE ANALYSIS

A simplified concept of accelerated proficiency is shown in figure 2, which depicts '*normal proficiency curve*' with a solid line and '*accelerated proficiency curve*' with a dotted line. Along the vertical axis is the hypothetical proficiency levels represented as P1 to P6. Certain assumptions are made in this representation. Though not everyone will be truly a novice in any job, for the sake of simplicity, in the context of a new job role, it may mean base level proficiency in new skills represented as P1. If nothing is done, an individual will start learning the skills required to do the new job at time N1 and may follow the normal proficiency curve, assuming a constant rate of proficiency

---

[2] Available at https://www.researchgate.net/publication/282648062

acquisition. Eventually, the individual will attain desired or target proficiency P4 in time N6. The time interval 'N6-N1' (measured from the start of the job) is called 'time to proficiency.'

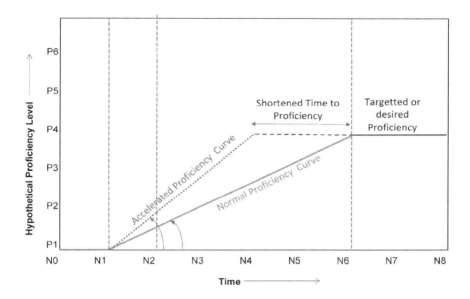

*Figure 2: Concept of accelerating time to proficiency: Accelerated Proficiency Curve (Copyrights Raman K. Attri)*

In a business context, the goal would be to reduce this time to proficiency, that is, time taken by employees to acquire desired proficiency. In other words, it would mean to raise the slope of the normal proficiency curve to a new slope represented by a dotted line as the accelerated proficiency curve. The efforts are made to raise the slope of this curve so that the other individuals in same job/role/ function may attain the same level of desire proficiency, P4, in a shorter time N4 (compared to N6). Instituting some deliberate, focused efforts to shorten this time is the goal of any *accelerated proficiency projects* in any organization.

Elemental analysis is done graphically on the graph shown in figure 2 using equations of a straight line, slope, and piece-wise representation. The graphic analysis shows that the accelerated proficiency curve could follow four possible but different routes to attain desired proficiency. These four routes are described in the following sections.

## 3.2    TRAJECTORY #1: ACCELERATED PROFICIENCY-BASED TRAINING

The first approach revealed by proficiency curve analysis is to continue training the learners independent of the amount of time involved, until desired proficiency is achieved. This approach assumes that training or learning should not end until that state is achieved.

**Approach**

The first route revealed by proficiency curve analysis is quite straight-forward, called 'proficiency-based training' approach. This approach is based on the scenario of what if an employee/learner is made to attend a program in which time is not a constraint, that is, a learner could receive training and move to next level by demonstrating competence rather than spending some specified time in that program. In such an arrangement, the learner would keep getting a series of formal training, learning assignments, continuous assessment/ feed-back, and support until s/he reaches the desired proficiency. In other words, the training/learning does not stop until s/he attains the desired proficiency level.

For such an intervention, the proficiency growth curve under normal circumstances is shown with a solid line in figure 3 as *conventional proficiency-based training curve*,' leading to desired proficiency in time N6. If some strategies could accelerate the slope of this curve to a new '*accelerated proficiency-based training curve,*' it might allow a learner to reach desired proficiency in a shorter time N4, compared to time N6, thus accelerating proficiency of that individual.

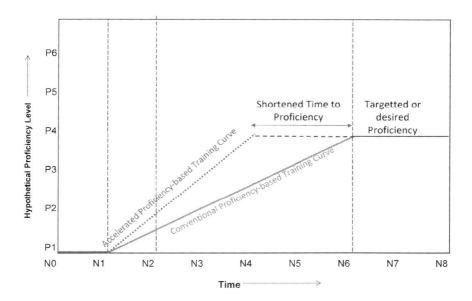

*Figure 3: Accelerated proficiency-based training approach (Copyrights Raman K. Attri)*

## Applications

Though the concept sounds impractical at first, this actually is based on Blooms' *Mastery Learning Approach,* in which the whole idea is to make trainees achieve proficiency in targeted skills during a training event by removing the time limits (Bloom 1968). The educational theorist Carroll (1963) provided the first complete model of attaining proficiency in her "Mastery learning model." Carroll challenged traditional educational philosophy with his model, stating that 'the learner will succeed in learning a given task to the extent that he spends

37

the time that he *needs* to learn the task' (Carroll 1963, p. 725). Carroll (1963) used certain factors like aptitude, the time needed to learn the task under ideal instruction, ability to understand instruction, perseverance, and external conditions like the time allowed for learning, and the quality of instruction. She speculated that the majority of learners would be successful in gaining mastery in learning by a suitable combination of these factors, and by systematically maximizing time allowed for learning.

Bloom (1968) further developed this theory with an experiment in which he argued that with the proper condition of learning and time given to learner, almost all learners were able to demonstrate desired performance. Inherently, this approach builds practice into its training philosophy. This is the fundamental premise of the proficiency-based training movement which supports the idea of continuing to allow the trainee to practice, until s/he has demonstrated desired standards of performance. Time is usually not a constraint in such a situation, but the mastery of some skills to a certain level is the target.

Proficiency-based training implies that it is possible to achieve a constant level of mastery across several learners and to make it independent of time or number of practice trials. Recently, several surgical and military educators have adopted the Blooms' Mastery Learning model to build employee proficiency right through training interventions. The training does not end until the desired proficiency is achieved. There are several studies that reported encouraging results with proficiency-based training mainly in surgical and laparoscopy applications (Angelo et al. 2015; Gallagher et al. 2005; Kolozsvari et al. 2011; Lee 2011; Nagel 2011; Rosenthal et al. 2009; Scott et al. 2008; Stefanidis et al. 2006; Wilcox et al. 2014). Pilot training has recently started using this methodology by lifting the restrictions on the same number of hours of practice for all trainees but to actually track progress by task (Stewart & Dohme 2005). Guskey (2009) cited several modern studies, which showed that mastery learning could be achieved on higher level learning goals (Arredondo & Block 1990; Blakemore 1992; Clark, Guskey, & Benninga 1983; Kozlovsky 1990; Mevarech 1980, 1981, 1985; Mevar-ech & Werner 1985; Soled 1987).

This approach would mean that even though an employee is not yet at full productivity level for every aspect of his job, s/he could still be competent to perform several functions of his job. Since the learner is continuously involved in on-the-job practice mode during the entire training cycle, organizations probably could use them for a specific part of the regular job.

## Implementation

In this approach, during the training cycle, the learner is engaged in learning and practice embedded together. It includes regular practice (like structured on-the-job S-OJT) or deliberate practice in which a learner is engaged in a repetitive performance, receives a rigorous assessment, and receives informative feedback (Ericsson et al. 1993). Proficiency metrics for training tasks can provide the external motivation necessary to engage them in the skills acquisition process in ways that are not merely passing the time or performing some arbitrary number of practice repetitions.

As of now, there are several research studies, mainly in surgical areas, which have demonstrated developing proficiency using a proficiency-based training approach. In some research studies, simulation has been demonstrated to accelerate the proficiency-based training approach.

## Flaws in this approach

This method has its challenges too. The first challenge with this approach is that it completely disregards any limit on the time needed to achieve the desired proficient level, hence faster time to proficiency is not even the purpose of believers of this philosophy. Such an approach at the educational institutions might work. However, it will be a hard sell to corporate managers telling them that time to proficiency could be unpredictable at best. It might be challenging for organizations to keep a newly hired employee "under-training" for an unpredictable amount of time, not knowing when he or she would reach desired proficiency. Additionally, this may risk employee engagement and a sense of achievement required to keep employees motivated.

In general, there is still a lack of research studies focusing on how time can be accelerated in a proficiency-based training approach itself. The reason is probably due to its philosophical origin of making training program "timeless" which would then be counter-intuitive to the attempt to 'accelerate' in any variation of this approach.

## 3.3 TRAJECTORY #2: ACCELERATED ON-THE-JOB EXPERIENCE

The second approach revealed by proficiency curve analysis is accelerating the on-the-job learning. It assumes that training has a limited contribution toward overall proficiency.

**Approach**

In general, most employees get some sort of training (typically classroom training) to start their job or a new role. This is shown with a solid line as *'conventional classroom training curve'* in figure 4.

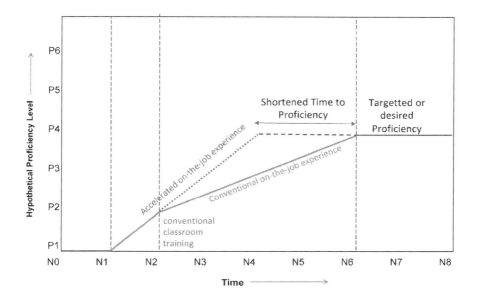

*Figure 4: Accelerated On-the-job Experience Approach (Copyrights Raman K. Attri)*

In most cases, this conventional/formal classroom training would not be more than a couple of weeks or so (depending upon the type of training of course). A new employee is provided with a systematic training event to learn the skills needed for the job. The training helps the novice to acquire the skills and attain a certain level of proficiency in the skills at the time of exit from the training course, say P2. The literature argues that traditionally, training prepares a novice only to attain a level called "advanced beginner" as defined by Dreyfus & Dreyfus's model (Clark 2008). Simply put, an advanced beginner is someone who starts comparing the new situations with previously experienced situations but still applies the earlier learned rules. Classroom training usually results in a spike in performance change and bring a novice to a level of advanced beginner.

41

What a novice lacks at the end of such a formal training program is the required experience, and time to practice the skills s/he learned in the training program. Therefore, after the learners finish their training, they are usually assigned to the job or projects where they perform things and learn on the job. Some of these arrangements may have formal on-the-job training (OJT) while others may have just informal job-shadowing. Employee learns several tasks during this phase at a rate which is determined by a number of cases or issues encountered, time available to practice and opportunities apply and further his skills. During this phase, the learning curve may take all sort of shapes and slopes depending on the person, job, situations, opportunities, and assignments. Steadily, learner acquires proficiency at a rate depicted by *conventional on-the-job experience curve* in figure 4. Depending on the rate of learning on-the-job individuals may reach desired proficiency eventually in time N4.

This approach suggests focusing solely on the on-the-job experience component of the proficiency curve. If there were some suitable strategies, it might be possible to shift the slope of 'conventional on-the-job experience curve' to a slope as in *accelerated on-the-job experience curve.*' It may be possible to reach desired proficiency in time N4 which is shorter than time N6 – thus, accelerating proficiency.

## Applications

A large number of companies heavily depend on on-the-job training as the primary approach to develop their employees. In one study by Rothwell & Kazanas (2004), it was revealed that 365 of managers believes on-the-job training is an essential part of a company's training strategy but do not know how to improve it. In a study by Barbian (2002), 77% of the leading companies in Training Magazine's Top 100 companies offer formal mentoring, 66% have job-shadowing programs, and 51% have job rotation programs. Lately, 70:20:10 model emphasized that 70% of the learning happen on the job and hence should be the critical focus of organizations toward accelerating proficiency. This may appear to be a common sense approach because most organizations rely on on-the-job experience to build the expertise of their employees.

An increasing number of jobs has shown that on-the-job experience is required to perform the job independently (i.e., proficiently). For example, to demonstrate proficiency to attain a license to fly a jet-powered commercial passenger airplane with a scheduled airline, a pilot needs an average 3000 flight hours of experience on-the-job (which include at least 1,500 hours' multi-engine, and at least 1000 hours as pilot in command) (Government Publishing Office 2013).

**Implementation**

Many corporations still use an informal or unplanned approach to OJT. As Filipczak (1993, p.30) explains, 'OJT has often meant having a new employee 'go sit by Nellie' or follow Sam around the factory floor playing monkey-see, monkey-do.' This is a case of unplanned OJT. However, the paradigm has shifted in the last couple of decades. Jacobs (2014) revisited a structured OJT (S-OJT) model which takes a system view on skills required by a newer staff to perform the job, systematically design shadowing to deliver experiences at the workplace, and checklists to evaluate it. Such structured on-the-job training interventions have been shown to accelerate employee readiness. More and more organizations have adopted such structured on-the-job training approaches to accelerate employee readiness, and some of them have reported a shorter time to productivity (Jacobs & Bu-Rahmah 2012; Jacobs 2014).

## Flaws in this approach

Most of the organizations have understood that on-the-job training, learning, and experience are critical to accelerating proficiency of employees. They tend to rely heavily on this newfound mechanism to build proficiency. In the process, they usually undermine the value of formal training, which might be necessary for initial readiness.

On-the-job learning period is indeed significantly more extended than classroom training. Though 'nothing can replace the field experience,' this approach leads to longer wait time for the right experience to present itself to the learner while on the job. Hoffman, Andrews & Feltovich (2012, p. 9) stated that 'A key factor which makes achieving the status of "expert" difficult is that typically, to be considered an "expert", an individual must be able to solve very difficult problems that most of their peers are not able to address.' A similar equation applies to developing a highly proficient employee. 'However, these types of problems are relatively rare, which makes learning by practice on the job problematic since they are seldom encountered' (Hoffman, Andrews & Feltovich 2012, p. 9). Sometimes it may take a really long time before someone is exposed to the events and acquire enough experience to become proficient. This is particularly true for complex problem-solving skills in which proficiency can only be acquired when an individual has acquired the refined schemata and mental representation which is possible only by working on several cases of a wide variety. As such, there is still an apparent lack of knowledge-base on how to accelerate on-the-job experience.

## 3.4    TRAJECTORY #3: RESTRUCTURED TRAINING CURRICULUM

The third approach revealed by proficiency curve analysis is to focus on restructuring the training curriculum in such a way that overall proficiency levels at the exit (or end of the training program) are uplifted while assuming that the learning that happens in the field is not easily controlled.

**Approach**

Conventional training curriculum has been in play for years as a pivotal mechanism to provide basic skills and knowledge to learners' and make them learn specific rules of the game on the job. With such traditional training courses, a novice is typically provided with rule-based guidelines and structure to give him the ability to apply these facts and figures into different situations. By definition, the learner attains proficiency of 'advanced beginner,' indicated as hypothetical proficiency level P2 in figure 5. Figure 5 shows a *'conventional classroom training curve'* which represents a block of training which typically happens within a reasonable time frame from N1 to N2.

Conceptually, one possibility is suggested by this graph to achieve the desired proficiency faster. What if training curriculum could be restructured to uplift the exit-proficiency level of the individual from being at 'advanced beginner' (P2) to at least a 'competent' (P3) level as per definition of Dreyfus & Dreyfus (1986). Such an approach would follow the trajectory shown by the *'restructured classroom training'* curve in figure 5. If we could lift the exit-proficiency level, s/he possesses much-refined knowledge and skills, and s/he would start his post-training assignments at a higher starting point of proficiency. The individual is likely to have a head-start for his on-the-job experience that is planned after his formal training. Assuming the same rate of skill acquisition as was in *'conventional on-the-job experience curve,'* an individual could achieve 'desired proficiency' in time N4, which is much faster than the original time to proficiency N6. Conceptually, this again leads to shortening time to proficiency, as shown in figure 5.

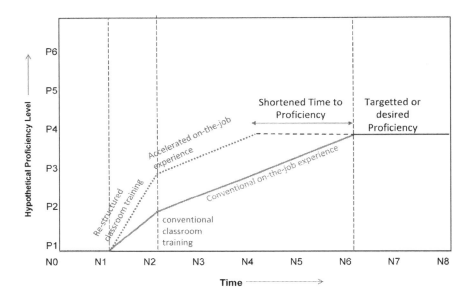

*Figure 5: Accelerating proficiency with restructured training approach (Copyrights Raman K. Attri)*

## Applications

With suitable instructional design techniques and instructional methods, the learner is developed into more competent than the learners who are put into the conventional route. The higher competence also means a better grasp of knowledge before the learner starts his on-the-job journey. According to literature, such pre-existing knowledge makes the learner to approach problems quickly and leverage previous mental representations to achieve expertise or proficiency faster (Chi, Glaser & Farr 1988). This leads a competent learner to learn at a faster rate, achieving 'desired proficiency' in a shorter time.

Several studies attempted to provide insight into how training can be used to "uplift" the proficiency of employees in a training event or a training program. Some famous models answer the question regarding the acceleration of proficiency. Some instructional design or training models support this approach. The model of intelligence proposed by Sternberg (1999) provides six training strategies to accelerate expertise. This model explains that metacognitive skills, learning skills, and thinking skills are the essential ingredients of lifting proficiency during training.

Clark (2008) specified cognitive strategies to build expertise through training. She presented a range of techniques starting from managing cognitive load to a part-task technique for building expertise, retention and skill practice, etc. Her compilation is one of the comprehensive efforts in proposing a range of training strategies drawn from previously well-established research studies as a solution to build a higher level of proficiency through training interventions.

The job roles are now becoming complex and increasingly requires learners to solve complex problems. To that effect, the restructured training approach focuses heavily on developing complex problem skills. Along similar lines, Hoffman et al. (2014) emphasized using tough cases to accelerate expertise through well-structured training. Hoffman et al. (2014) specified a range of case studies and past research studies on how training should be restructured to accelerate expertise toward high proficiency. Proposing a similar stand of using tough cases, DiBello & Missildine (2008, 2011, 2013) proposed a strategy of simulating rapid failures in a compressed timeframe to accelerate proficiency rapidly.

**Implementation**

Under this premise, the employee is developed to exit at a higher level of proficiency right during the training course. This proficiency is achieved with a curriculum training structure loaded with real-life scenarios, thinking intensive exercises, complex problem-solving and emotional loading. Such instructional design techniques provide learners with abilities such as sophisticated information processing, better mental knowledge representation, skills in chunking information, speedy pattern recognition and highly developed metacognitive skills, to a certain extent, which are all characteristics of the expert performer (Dror 2011).

**Flaws in this approach**

This approach basically is a simple and intuitive concept of how focusing on training intervention has many rewarding effects allowing organizations to build a certain level of proficiency within the training programs and attaining the desired proficiency faster. Though it can provide initial readiness at the job, several experts commonly believe that classroom training never leads to proficiency. Also, the new philosophies like 70:20:10 tend to assert that structured and formal training is not the key to proficiency (Jennings & Wargnier 2010). On the other hand, the believers of structure training like Six Disciplines of Training (Pollock, Wick & Jefferson 2015), warn that initial training is a vital piece of the equation for success at the workplace.

Nevertheless, this approach suggests that training intervention needs to be restructured in such a way to build a significant portion of proficiency during training. However, it may mean a much longer training duration than otherwise required by other traditional models.

## 3.5 TRAJECTORY #4: HOLISTIC PICTURE TO ACCELERATE PROFICIENCY

While each of the three approaches discussed in previous sections has some merits, it would be reasonable to think that none of those approaches are complete in itself. To develop and accelerate proficiency holistically, one has to merge all the three approaches, to develop a new trajectory shown with a dotted line in figure 6.

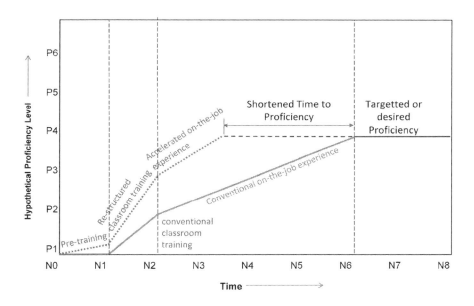

*Figure 6: Combining multiple approaches into one to accelerating proficiency (Copyrights Raman K. Attri)*

Conceptually, there are three possibilities to achieve a shorter time to proficiency if an individual is made to follow the path depicted by red dotted lines in three trajectories explained earlier:

- First, provide pre-training learning of some basic skills before new hires are assigned into any instructor-led training. Raise his proficiency level slightly compared to the initial proficiency P0.
- Second, get new hire started with his instructor-led training or classroom training with a slightly higher level of proficiency that gives him a head-start. This likely raises his learning curve during ILT class and likely enable him with higher proficiency than P1.
- Third, with a higher level of exit-proficiency, s/he is likely to be more successful at accelerating his on-the-job learning. Such accelerated learning (achieved by making entry-level proficiency higher) may lead him to reach the desired proficiency level P3 in a much shorter time.

The key driving factor to integrate three trajectories into one would be the analysis of the inventory of skills, knowledge, behaviors, and nature of tasks to be supported in a new job role. Once the inventory of ingredients to attain desired business goals for the stated role are defined, then it is a matter of proper analysis to understand what skills must be learned via online learning, what can be delivered through formal training, what must be experienced on-the-job, and what can be supported with tools like performance support systems (PSS).

Part of this analysis also would tell what skills are pre-requisites and individuals should either be hired for those skills or they should be provided all the content and other self-learning support that potentially can get them started with some heads-up before they attend a formal training program. Using such a 'pre-training' approach, the rate of learning/proficiency acquisition during restructured training could be much higher, and this may give the advantage to accelerate the on-the-job experience curve further. If the amount of head-start (i.e., "lift") is appropriately supported, it may even be possible for an individual to attain desired proficiency in a time shorter than N4 (Attri & Wu 2016a, 2016b). Further, balancing classroom training vs. on-the-job interventions, one could accelerate proficiency significantly.

Combining various approaches to accelerate proficiency also means that there cannot be such sharp boundaries between training and on-the-job experience. Both components have to work together. Training interventions need to be redesigned or restructured in such a way that develops a significant portion of desired proficiency during the training event itself. Such an effort will uplift the exit level proficiency of employees. On the other hand, organizations need to implement several non-training strategies alongside training strategies, to embed on-the-job experience and formal training together. One needs to come up with different ways to incorporate on-the-job experience in the formal training structure itself or situate training into the day-to-day work on the job. Striking a balance between formal training and on-job-experience in a reasonable period is one of the several central issues in the study about time to proficiency. Further, on-the-job experience needs to be designed, monitored and mentored accurately.

The strategies and practices to implement such a holistic approach require a proficiency eco-system that supports every aspect of developing and accelerating proficiency (Attri & Wu 2017; 2018). This holistic model of eco-system is out of the scope of this book[3]. This book will focus on four trajectories within the realms of training and learning design.

---

[3] Interested readers can see: Attri, RK & Wu, WS 2018, "Model of accelerated proficiency in the workplace: six core concepts to shorten time-to-proficiency of employees," *Asia Pacific Journal of Advanced Business and Social Studies*, vol. 4, no. 1, http://dx.doi.org/10.25275/apjabssv4i1bus1.

## 3.6 SIMPLIFIED REPRESENTATION OF FOUR PHASES

The proficiency curve analysis suggested four different trajectories to accelerate proficiency. The four different representations of accelerated proficiency suggested four possible, but distinct segments of blocks of time which are akin to phases. These phases represent a specific type of learning activities that take place in that segment. The segments are N0 to N1, N1 to N2, N2 to N4 (accelerated) or N2 to N6 (traditional) shown in figure 7. Viewing these segments as phases is the most simplistic, minimalistic representation of how one progresses toward the targeted proficiency, though we know individuals take several different paths to attain required proficiency (shown in figure 7 with thin solid lines). Based on the nature of learning activities, these phases are described as follows. The chapters that follow will reference the learning activities to these phases.

**Pre-instructor-led training (Pre-ILT) phase:** In a typical scenario, at the workplace, a new hire is brought into the organization at time N0 with some base proficiency P0 (let us assume) for the job. S/he is provided some onboarding orientation. During this orientation, the new hire typically would read or undergo some organizational processes not particular to the job. Technically, the new hires are not learning specific skills of their job. There tends to be a "bench time" which may vary from one job to another. This bench period is from N0 to N1. This phase is termed as *pre-instructor-led training (Pre-ILT) phase* in figure 7.

**Instructor-led training (ILT) phase:** Most technical organizations have job-specific training that is offered to new employees. In most cases, this training is instructor-led/classroom-based training specific to imparting product knowledge, specific skills to do the job function and processing that are used during that job role. Usually, this period from N1 to N2 may be spread into multiple ILT sessions, depending on the nature of the job. Typically, a new employee could see a small uplift in his proficiency to do the new job to a level P1. This phase is termed as *Instructor-led training (ILT) phase* in figure 7.

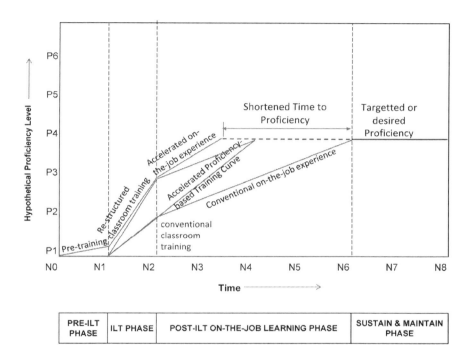

*Figure 7: Four phases of proficiency acquisition in typical training-oriented settings (Copyrights Raman K. Attri)*

**Post-ILT on-the-job learning phase:** From there on, they are on the job, performing various activities with someone or independently. Some organizations tend to have parallel mentoring, coaching or on-the-job training to provide an individual with more experience to do the job. With repeated assignments and involvement in various activities, an individual may learn at a certain rate and eventually reaches desired proficiency P3 defined for the job in a time interval N6-N2. The total time, N6, taken by an individual to reach desired proficiency, called time to proficiency, may be very long depending on several factors. This phase is termed as *Post-ILT on-the-job learning phase.*

With conscious efforts, the traditional proficiency curve can be accelerated, and an individual may attain desired proficiency in a shorter time, say N4. The post-ILT on-the-job learning phase then runs up to N4.

**Sustain and maintain phase:** If the individual is continuously engaged in job-specific assignments at a higher rate, s/he will maintain that level of proficiency. This is termed the sustain and maintain phase which starts from the time an individual reaches desired proficiency N6 or earlier.

# CHAPTER 4

# FOUR TYPES OF INEFFICIENCIES IN TRAINING HAMPER ACCELERATED PROFICIENCY

Before we discuss training-related findings in *the TTP study,* it is important to discuss whether or not today's training strategies used by the organizations contribute toward accelerating proficiency. The 85 project leaders who participated in *the TTP study* were asked: In their experience, what is the role of training models in supporting or hindering the acceleration of proficiency? The responses from over 66 projects cases showed that in the organizations, there are situations when training intervention in some form is the best solution to provide the necessary skills for a given job role.

However, almost all the project leaders also shared a range of bottlenecks and hindrances which came on the way to accelerating the proficiency when training is used as the primary mechanism. The purpose of this chapter is to describe findings on various challenges and inefficiencies noted during the analysis.

## 4.1 WHAT IS WRONG WITH A TYPICAL TRADITIONAL TRAINING MODEL

Before proceeding, it is vital to explain the traditional training model with an example. A project leader gave a relevant account of a typical traditional model.

**Project No. 59:** For a job role of financial services executive engaged in upselling of financial products higher up to the executive line, traditional training approach before any initiative to shorten time-to-proficiency was put in place, and looked like this:

*"Though when I arrived on site, we did an analysis of their training program. And what we learned was that they would spend about six weeks in a classroom-based experience that literally was about fifty-fifty turned on lecture and then hands-on use of the IT tools at their place. But the real challenge was that there was no expectation of the employee to pass any type of assessment, or to measure, to have anything measurable at all. Picture that world [sic] that you could sit in this room for six weeks and sleep during [the] class, and at the end of the day, you were able to survive the six weeks. ... What value were you really getting from these folks when they finished their training? And now they go up the next phase of their program, which was an on the job coaching program. ...*

*So as part of the problem that we looked at, we identified that classroom training itself did not have any foundation. So there weren't lots of plans or any type of structured guides. It was primarily one-way. ... So it could change drastically from instructor to instructor.*

*Then finally, there wasn't enough hands-on usage of the tools, so a lot of times they would come out of the classroom and they wouldn't even be doing any observation. But when they finished their training program, they have forgotten what they learned in the classroom and almost had to re-learn how to use technology. There was more focus in the classroom on the product than the technology that was being used.*

*And the third part was they learned that the coaches themselves in the second part [on-the-job] part] of the program never changed. So if we had somebody who was getting bitter or using this as a way of not being on the phone [and] was rather as a side effect of "Okay, I do this, I don't have to take customer calls." There was a gap in terms of being able to properly coach employees on what to do in certain situations"* [Project Leader].

Other project cases exhibited similar accounts of training models which organizations were using, and these models were analyzed for patterns on why those were not leading to accelerated proficiency. Such a model was deemed as "copied from the academic world to corporate settings." Invariably, analysis of every project case led to the observations that some inefficiencies in the traditional or conventional training models either hampered shortening time to proficiency or were the leading cause of a long time to proficiency. There was little to no evidence on if and how traditional training models supported, enabled or speeded up the proficiency.

It was postulated that traditional training models (particularly taken from academic settings, like the one described above) do not really lead to accelerating the proficiency; instead, such models add to longer time to proficiency problem.

From the analysis, four categories of challenges or inefficiencies in traditional training models emerged. The conceptual map shown in figure 8 summarizes the challenges or inefficiencies of most of the commonly used traditional training models. These four categories are a) Curriculum design-related inefficiencies; b) Skill-related inefficiencies;

c) Support-related inefficiencies; d) Outcomes-related inefficiencies. These four main categories were developed from over 15 significant patterns, which in turn were developed from combining over 100 themes across the project cases. The scale of *the TTP study* led to several inefficiencies in training models for the first time, which was not the primary goal of the study, and which probably warrants a separate detailed publication. For this chapter, each category is described briefly.

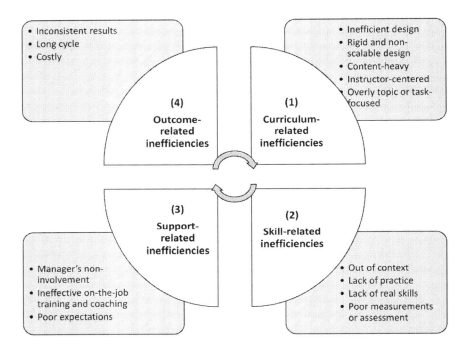

*Figure 8: Conceptual map of four types of inefficiencies in traditional training models (Copyrights Raman K. Attri)*

## 4.2 INEFFICIENCY #1: CURRICULUM-RELATED INEFFICIENCIES

Data analysis suggests that traditional organizational training programs are suffering from five curriculum-related challenges – Inefficient design, Rigid and non-scalable design, Content-heavy, Instructor-centered, Overly topic or task-focused. Main inefficiencies patterns emerged in this category are summarized in table 3 and are briefly described here.

**Inefficient Design:** Major tendency noted was regarding inefficient design. It was seen from the analysis that most of the training specialists adopted or copied the typical "academic way" of designing training programs into corporate settings using obsolete learning theories not applicable anymore in workplace settings. This academic style instructional design assumed that training was the only solution in a given situation. With that assumption, the training departments and learning specialists typically entrusted with this job usually start with massive task analysis that leads to defining performance objectives in terms of activities and tasks, as opposed to performance analysis in an attempt to define proficiency in terms of business outcomes. Starting with over-detailed task analysis and too much focus on breaking tasks into sub-components leads to a lengthy list of skills, sub-skills, knowledge, and behaviors, etc. 'It is very difficult because the training department was starting with job descriptions, with job positions, with job skills. They were starting with task analysis of the cashier, for example. … they are assuming that the cashier needs all the training. They let them go through the entire process. That is what you call the typical task-analysis type of learning' [project leader]. Not all of the identified sub-skills directly address the real challenges of a long time to proficiency at the workplace and does not directly equip the learners on how to attain expected business outcomes.

*Table 3: Curriculum-related challenges of traditional training*

| Major inefficiency | Themes |
| --- | --- |
| INEFFICIENT DESIGN | Academic way |
| | Cumbersome job analysis |
| | Enforced preset design on the learning of learners |
| | Focus on short-term gains only |
| | Informally trained |
| | Linear path |
| | Mismanaged informal learning |
| | old learning theories |
| | Poor design |
| | Poor retention |
| | Qualitative decisions on content |
| | Redundancy |
| | Tools geared toward formal training |
| | Traditional format copied to e-learning |
| | Unstructured |
| | Unstructured documentation or procedures |
| | wastage of time |
| | Wrong data analytics |
| RIGID AND NON-SCALABLE | Institutionalized rigid structure |
| | Non-scalability |
| | Non-scalable cognitive apprenticeship model |
| | One-size-fits-all |
| CONTENT HEAVY | Content-centered |
| | Dump content upfront |
| | Information overload |
| | Irrelevant information |
| | "Just-in-case" content |
| | Massive content |
| | Old obsolete content |
| | Over-teaching |
| INSTRUCTOR-CENTERED | Classroom obsession |
| | Instructor-centric |
| | One-way lectures |
| TOPIC OR TASK-FOCUSED | Task-oriented |
| | Too task-focused training |
| | Topic-based curriculum |
| | Traditional case studies as an addendum |

**Rigid and non-scalable design:** Above tendency appears to lead to next issue of a very rigid and non-scalable training program which are overly structured to the point that it tried to force-fit institutions' inflexible one-size-fits-all solution philosophy. 'So basically [as] an engineer regardless of what the issue that he encounters, that you would be "prepared" to support it, kind of a one-size-fits-all approach' [project leader]. Ultimately such emphasis on overly formal training programs loses focus on the expected job outcomes.

**Content-heavy**: Almost all the project leaders indicated that the major challenge they faced in the old training model was that the curriculum was too content-centric or content heavy, and loaded with slides, irrelevant or non-contextual information. The tendency was to load all kinds of content including 'just-in-case' which leads to over-stuffed and fatty training programs. 'There's no way that this learner is going to remember all of this content. ... we were teaching people how to do something, how to handle a call that they may get one or two of those calls a year, and they'll never remember it when that call finally comes' [project leader]. The net result is a lengthy training course or program which may run for weeks depending on job or content. Such massive content does not allow enough practice on the required skills.

**Instructor-centered**: Most of the traditional training programs were heavily instructor-centered, in which instructor's job had been to download the content for the learners through one-way lectures typically in the classroom settings without the real application of the skills being in the training. Training is supposed to be done when the instructor has covered the content or course objectives. 'In the old version of the program, it was a lot of lectures. You had somebody standing in front of the room talking and sometimes demonstrating how to fulfill something, and then we would turn them loose to work on it' [project leader]. Such a design leads to poor retention and skills learned in a training program are not transferred to the workplace.

61

**Overly topic or task-focused:** The result was another issue that the curriculum so developed was organized as a topic-wise-topic sequence to enable training delivery rather than structuring how the job was being done. 'They're often left with a big fat ring binder with all that stuff in it, and that is almost useless because it's organized around a training course, not around the way the job is done' [project leader].

## 4.3 INEFFICIENCY #2: SKILL-RELATED INEFFICIENCIES

Analysis indicated that traditional training models suffered from four challenges in enabling learners to apply their skills. These challenges are - lack of real skills, out of context training, limited practice, poor measurement or assessment of skills. Main patterns of inefficiencies that emerged in this category are summarized in table 4 and are briefly described here.

**Out of context:** Analysis noted that conventional training solutions took the people away from the job and the context in which they were supposed to work. 'The person reading it didn't know what part he or she was responsible for doing and what part somebody else on the team might do and who that person might be' [project leader]. When the people are taken away from the context, the transfer of skills learned in the classroom out of context does not transfer back easily to the context.

**Lack of practice:** Though several organizations were seen using case-based and simulation-based approaches, those approaches focused heavily on meeting the learning objectives of the course and hence were designed with a very limited number of practice sessions. 'There was a lot of "Watch me do this." And then very limited "Okay, your turn, you do it' [project leader]. Also, the simulated practice was mostly focused on the repetition of the everyday tasks. Such a design did not prepare learners with enough practice on low-frequency events which may become catastrophic at some time in the future.

*Table 4: Skill-related challenges of traditional training*

| Major inefficiency | Themes |
| --- | --- |
| OUT OF CONTEXT | Away from job |
| | No context |
| LIMITED PRACTICE | Lack of opportunities to practice on low-frequency emergencies |
| | Limited exposure and opportunities |
| | Little practice on low frequency |
| | No time to transfer knowledge |
| | Rapid skill decay |
| | Too little investment and efforts |
| LACK OF REAL SKILLS | Challenges with simulators |
| | Gaps between skill-sets required in the field vs. taught in class |
| | Generic and specific skills packed in instructor-led training |
| | Lack of business skills |
| | lack of confidence to deal with complexity |
| | Lack of integration skills |
| | Lack of thinking moments |
| | Lack of troubleshooting skills |
| | Unrealistic levels of skills |
| | Unrealistic time pressure |
| POOR MEASUREMENTS OR ASSESSMENT | Ineffective assessment |
| | Lack of measurement |
| | Traditional paper pen assessment |

**Lack of real skills:** Even contextually well-designed training programs lacked the realistic skills required to achieve the desired proficiency at the workplace. Most programs also lacked skills toward integration, problem-solving, thinking and business skills required to address increasing complexity and dynamism of the unpredictable workplace challenges. 'People do a lot of things with – they also do them in combinations and a lot of times when you don't teach things together [but in] pieces and parts; the people never figure out how to do it together' [project leader].

**Poor measurements or Assessment:** Learners were typically not given clear accountabilities and expectations. The assessment criteria for measurements were generally poorly defined. There was that there was no expectation of the employee to pass any type of assessment, or to measure, [or] to have anything measurable at all' [project leader]. It is seen that the training department typically focused on meeting the course objectives successfully in which 'success' was tested using typical paper and pen type assessments, rather than with the actual on-the-job deliverables.

## 4.4    INEFFICIENCY #3: SUPPORT-RELATED INEFFICIENCIES

The analysis noted that conventional training programs lacked provision of required support to learners before and after training in three areas - ineffective on-the-job training and coaching, manager's non-involvement and poor expectations set up for a given training. Main inefficiencies patterns are summarized in table 5 and are briefly described here.

**Manager's non-involvement:** Analysis suggested that in most of the project cases managers had thought of training intervention as a 'magic' which could instantly produce a proficient employee without requiring any effort or attention from the managers. Therefore, managers tended not to typically get involved during training design or delivery or any such discussions. 'There are instances where trainees will attend training, come back and try to do what they were taught, and the manager says, "That's not how we do it here." And so, anytime you have that disconnect between training and what goes on in the field, or how the managers in the field think it should be done, that clearly is going to decelerate time-to-proficiency' [project leader]. The problem of developing proficient employees was left pretty much to the training department folks, who in turn ended up applying their instructional design or learning design skills, stayed disconnected from the real expectations of field proficiency as well as from the time to proficiency targets.

*Table 5: Support-related challenges of traditional training*

| Major inefficiency | Themes |
|---|---|
| INEFFECTIVE OJT AND COACHING | Bad behavior from senior workers |
| | certification describes only knowledge and skills |
| | Coaching not aligned with training |
| | The inconsistency of OJT trainers |
| | inconsistent and variations in methods |
| | Incorrect sign-off |
| | Manager's lack of support to assign top performer to coach |
| | Mentor and mentee cultural differences |
| | no monitoring of OJT and proficiency attainment in the field |
| | The old model of classroom plus OJT |
| | The traditional method of job-shadowing |
| MANAGER'S NON-INVOLVEMENT | Lack of a manager's follow-up |
| | Manager as an ineffective coach |
| | No involvement of the manager |
| | Supervisors lack accountability |
| POOR EXPECTATIONS | Lack of self-drive or initiative of learners |
| | No time factor in expectations |
| | Poor training transfer |
| | Significant variations in incoming skills |

**Ineffective on-the-job training and coaching:** Even at the workplace, the support given to learners from their mentors is either lacking or unstructured. The traditional method of job-shadowing is 'Go and watch Joe' without much accountability on the part of the learner, mentor, and the manager. Mentors were not aligned with training program objectives, and they were not given any metrics to measure the new learners on. Changing mentors or coaches resulted in the inconsistent learning experience and impacted the rate at which a learner could achieve proficiency. 'If the trainee was instructed, "Go and watch Joe on how to operate this filter pump." If Joe wasn't available and [to] the trainee again the supervisor said, "Go and watch Charlie on how to operate the filter pump." You couldn't expect necessarily that Joe and Charlie taught the procedure the same way' [project leader].

**Poor expectations**: It is also noted that in the absence of coaching and support, learners lacked self-drive or initiative. Lack of practice coupled with it led to the poor transfer of skills at the workplace. The major issue noticed in the traditional training was that there was no expectations or time set, and this resulted in a longer time to learn. 'There was no sense of urgency or expectation, there was no performance expectation set prior to this, and there was no follow-up to-- there were no ramifications if they did it or didn't do it before' [project leader].

## 4.5 INEFFICIENCY #4: OUTCOME-RELATED INEFFICIENCIES

The analysis noted that traditional training models suffered from poor results and outcomes. Three major issues noticed are - inconsistent results, a long cycle of readiness, and is costly. Main inefficiencies patterns are summarized in table 6 and are briefly described here.

*Table 6: Outcome-related challenges of traditional training*

| Major inefficiency | Themes |
| --- | --- |
| INCONSISTENT RESULTS | Inconsistent outcome and customer experience |
| | Variations in time-to-proficiency |
| LONG CYCLE | The inertia of training development |
| | Long time to proficiency |
| | Long training cycle |
| | long wait time between instructor-led sessions |
| | Slow speed |
| COSTLY | Expensive |
| | Low ROI |
| | Resource intensive |
| | Travel |
| | underutilized resources |

**Inconsistent results:** All of the issues mentioned in the previous three categories resulted in a critical problem that there was usually no indication of the time mark of when an individual had attained the desired proficiency. All these factors and challenges collectively led to inconsistent results, variations in time to proficiency of individuals, which was even harder to measure. 'Too Much Variation in time to competence' [project leader].

**Long Cycle:** Ultimately it led to slow speed with which people could be made ready for their job. 'It was taking them about a year to do that. So there were three months in sort of training, and then it was taking them an additional nine months to reach that score' [project leader]. Part of the factor was the long time taken to develop the training programs which slowed down the skill acquisition and resulted in a longer time to proficiency.

**Costly:** Hastening speed becomes a very resource intensive project when multiple instructors are engaged to add capacity, or when over-teaching of content is involved. '[Learners] need to be here for 3 months working in our little mockup facility, and we would have to spend a huge amount of money on our equipment to get it to the operational level' [project leader]. However, the focus remained on preparing people primarily through training and learning interventions, which required travel and hence added to costs.

## 4.6 HANDLING INEFFICIENCIES OF TRADITIONAL TRAINING MODELS

The pattern analysis across 66 projects revealed four categories of inefficiencies, leading to 15 different challenges and over 100 indicators of inefficiencies with which the traditional training model suffered across all project cases and all job roles. These inefficiencies hampered the speed to proficiency.

The analysis of *the TTP study* recognized that the value of training might be limited to traditional business goals of performance improvement, skill development and to provide initial operating readiness to the people on the job. However, one needs to address several critical inefficiencies of traditional training models to design training interventions in such a way that would support the goal of shortening time to proficiency. A different kind of training model and a different set of strategies are required when the goal is to reduce time to proficiency with high reliance on workplace activities.

The chapters that follow reveals the promising strategies found in this research study in regards to e-learning design (Chapter 5), classroom instructions (Chapter 6), and workplace learning (Chapter 7).

# FIVE E-LEARNING STRATEGIES TO ACCELERATE PROFICIENCY[4]

E-learning has made big waves in the past decade. E-learning definition changes with endless possibilities every new electronic technology bring for driving learning  Kahiigi Kigozi et al. (2008). A long time ago, computer-based training was deemed as e-learning while in most recent time virtual reality is considered to be a new face of e-learning. No doubt that e-learning has emerged as one of the most attractive and cost-effective solutions with the flexibility to support self-paced learning which can be delivered geographically to any place

---

[4] A version of this chapter was presented as a conference paper: Attri, RK & Wu, WS 2016, "E-learning strategies at workplace that support speed to proficiency in complex skills," in M Rozhan and N Zainuddin (eds.), *Proceedings of the 11th International Conference on E-Learning: ICEl2016*, Kuala Lampur, 2-3 June, Academic Conference and Publishing, Reading, pp. 176–184, available at <https://www.researchgate.net/publication/303802961>.

on the earth. A survey by Elearningindustry.com in 2014 reported that over 47% of the Fortune 500 companies now use some form of educational technology and corporations value e-learning as the second most valuable training method which saves business at least 50% cost when they replace traditional classroom training with e-learning (Pappas 2013). According to the ASTD State of the Industry Report, 38% of the training is delivered using technology-based solutions (ASTD 2014). The report also cited an IBM report stating that companies employing e-Learning have the potential to boost productivity by 50%. According to their estimates, every $1 spent on e-learning results in $30 productivity (ASTD 2014).

However, there is some caveat to these trends. Most of the organizations have not been able to harness the power of e-learning fully beyond one-way informational content. Therefore, it is imperative to investigate contributions or role of e-learning toward accelerating time to proficiency of the workforce, particularly for accelerating complex cognitive skills.

This chapter intends to describe five e-learning design strategies that were found to be promising toward accelerating time to proficiency. This chapter also describes the preliminary conceptual model that emerged out of the initial analysis in *the TTP study*. The findings were presented at the International Conference on E-learning (ICEL), Kuala Lumpur in a paper titled '*E-learning Strategies at Workplace That Support Speed to Proficiency in Complex Skills.*'

## 5.1   ROLE OF E-LEARNING IN ACCELERATING PROFICIENCY

Jobs are becoming increasingly complex in the workplace. A task as simple as 'calling a customer' has now become over-complex with considerations such as the ability to hold the client's attention, cultural and situational sensitivity to a customer's surroundings, ability to connect and relate with a customer's needs not just in the business sense but in socio-cultural sense too; ability to think through options and be able to research certain information for the customer. Karoly & Panis (2004) emphasize that the changing nature of the workplace requires non-routine cognitive skills. Complex cognitive skills require a different kind of design or approach. It is a general belief that face-to-face instructor-led and on-the-job mentored training have proven its potential in developing complex skills in the workplace as well as in educational or training provider's settings. However, e-learning's ability to deliver and accelerate highly complex cognitive skills has been debated extensively. There are indeed some examples of highly interactive e-learning solutions which boast of delivering (and accelerating) complex cognitive knowledge and skills in any complex job.

Many researchers have even questioned whether or not e-learning is plausible media to deliver complex cognitive skills. E-learning also gets questioned about its 'stickiness' or effectiveness in transferring skills to the workplace, particularly for complex skills. (Sims et al. 2008, p. 24) state that 'In fact, a common criticism of e-learning is that face-to-face courses are directly transferred to an electronic format with the assumption that the courses will be equally effective and accepted by trainees.' It appears that e-learning fails to deliver results when designers get into a trap of using principles meant for simpler skills to design e-learning for complex skills. The reality of this is probbaly revealed by Wulf & Shea (2002, p. 185) in their study which argued that 'principles derived from the study of simple skills do not generalize to complex skill learning.' They further emphasized that complex skills indicate the need to approach the learning of complex and simple skills differently. For example, learning simple skills profits from an 'increase in load' whereas the learning of complex skills requires 'reduction in load.' The point here is that e-learning targeted to develop highly complex cognitive skills need a different set of strategies.

With the pace of technology, the time-to-market pressures are changing demands on the workforce to acquire complex skills at a faster pace. Only a few of the research studies give some evidence or guidelines to design e-learning that could accelerate expertise or time to proficiency. Some industry figures substantiate the fact that e-learning holds the potential to accelerate proficiency. According to statistics reported by Pappas (2013) at Elearningindustry.com, e-learning cuts down the instruction time by 60%, increased information retention rates by 60% and compared to classroom learning; e-learning students are reported to have 60% faster learning curve. Though this evidence is mostly commercial in nature based on a limited set of surveys, the value of e-learning technologies, platforms, and methods cannot be denied in regards to its ability to cut down training length, allow self-paced learning and reinforcement to traditional training methods (Clark & Mayer 2011; Zhang 2005).

Lately, several researchers have proposed different strategies by which e-learning could be designed or administrated to develop complex skills of the learners. This study's preliminary findings suggested five e-learning curriculum design strategies that could potentially shorten time to proficiency.

## 5.2   CONCEPTUAL MODEL OF E-LEARNING STRATEGIES

The analysis of the themes that emerged in *the TTP study* revealed the following five major e-learning strategies that hold strong potential to accelerate speed to proficiency:

1. **Experience-rich multi-technology mix** - Which e-learning channel or technology can deliver intended skill to provide enriched experience and deeper learning?

2. **Time-spaced microlearning conten**t - Which skill can be packed in shorter e-learning units that can be applied immediately at the job?

3. **Scenario-based contextualization of e-learning** - Which task requires more in-depth thinking and solving a range of problems to achieve business outcomes?

4. **On-demand electronics performance support systems (EPSS)** - Which skills can be delivered through PSS to provide just-in-time (JIT) support at the moment of need?

5. **Optimally sequenced e-learning path** – Which e-learning activities would make someone reach proficiency quickly and which activities do not lead to proficiency?

Based on initial data patterns, it was hypothesized that time to proficiency of employees can be shortened if organizations develop a shorter chunk of content; contextualize it with real-world problems relevant to the workplace; sequence and organize the chunks in an optimally designed learning path; deliver each chunk virtually or online using several technologies, and making it available through electronic performance systems.

Subsequently, a conceptual model was developed as shown in figure 9. This conceptual model depicts the relationship between five e-learning strategies. The five e-learning strategies are tied to each other in a closed-loop and interact with each other seamlessly to accelerate proficiency in an integrated fashion. The way one strategy is implemented could significantly impact the effectiveness of the other strategies, by supplementing or complementing each other. The bi-directional arrows show such interaction in figure 9.

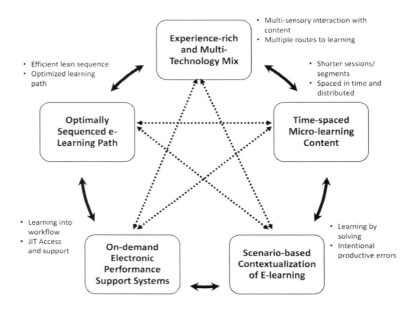

*Figure 9: Conceptual model of e-learning for accelerated proficiency (Copyrights Raman K. Attri)*

The conceptual model is expanded further in figure 10 with meta questions that are asked at each node to guide the instructional design. The resulting e-learning curriculum contributes better toward accelerated proficiency goals if all the five e-learning strategies are woven together to a certain degree.

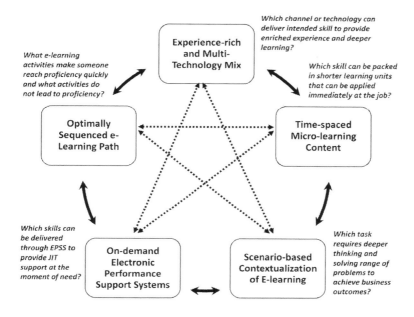

*Figure 10: Meta questions for five e-learning strategies to accelerate proficiency (Copyrights Raman K. Attri)*

## 5.3    STRATEGY #1: EXPERIENCE-RICH AND MULTI-TECHNOLOGY MIX

Early on Bower et al. (2015, p. 15) had predicted that 'Ideally in the years to come, rich-media collaborative technologies will become so invisible that students and teachers interacting from different locations will feel as though they are in the same room.' With recent tremendous technological advances in smart and mobile technologies, new channels of blended learning have opened up which includes virtual and remote classrooms. In an earlier study, Sims et al. (2008, p. 26) suggested such 'a blended learning approach may be more effective than a training session that relies completely on one mode or strategy.'

The findings in *the TTP study* showed similar results that by providing multiple experience-rich channels of information and content delivery to match the learning styles of the diverse workforce, organizations could cut the time to readiness. Learning designers in *the TTP study* were seen using several tools and channels of information delivery to enrich the learning, such as social media, remote presentations, real-time messengers, video portals, online books, peer-to-peer coaching, discussion forums, project work or fieldwork, etc. The cases reported that the latest technologies (like CISCO Telepresence, Google Hangout or YouTube streaming) offered powerful interactions virtually, rich experience and multiple channels of learning. Use of multiple enriched channels extended interactions beyond instructor to the peers and others, 'that isn't just delivering the same content we could deliver about in a classroom ... You're looking at something that's much, much more powerful' [project leader]. Several project leaders also mentioned that lending newer e-learning technologies could enrich virtual training sessions that allow multi-sensory interaction with the content, and caters to different preferences and requirements of the learners. 'Whereby using technology and making a combination of virtual and live classes ... has allowed it [accelerated learning] to scale more efficiently and happen in a faster time frame' [project leader].

The majority of the project leaders mentioned that these virtual classrooms are actually more effective than a traditional classroom because it allowed not only good face time but also extended interactions beyond instructor to peers and others: 'By the nature of the training being virtual, the format was different and more interactive than it was in a traditional classroom environment' [project leader]. Previous studies also supported that virtual classrooms are more effective than traditional classrooms in some cases. For example, Bower et al. (2015) demonstrated that various technologies like web conferencing, video conferencing, and the virtual world makes learning highly active with positive feedback from students. Similarly, Yilmaz (2015) showed that students who attended live virtual lectures achieved significantly higher scores as compared to the group who watched only the recorded sessions. It appears that these new technology channels if integrated into an existing blended learning model can take learning to an entirely new level.

Collectively, multiple channels provided several learning routes to employees, cutting overall time to proficiency significantly.

**Design guidelines**

- Include a broader scope and definition of e-learning while designing channels of information.
- Use media rich channels which allow hands-on experience and multi-sensory processing of information.
- Use multiple channels for delivery of the same information or use multiple formats of the same information and allow learners to be able to learn via any of the formats or modes.
- Leverage latest technologies like mobile learning, virtual reality, augmented reality, video conference, remote sharing and others which allow more interactions.

## 5.4   STRATEGY #2: TIME-SPACED MICROLEARNING CONTENT

Data analysis in *the TTP study* showed that technology-driven virtual training sessions become more effective when splitting into shorter sessions, with each session focused on a few learning outcomes at a time. This strategy has been discussed in the literature as 'chunking,' 'bite-size learning' (Mayer & Moreno 2003), 'microlearning' (Hug, Lindner & Bruck 2006), or 'segmenting' (Clark and Mayer 2011).

Microlearning is a more contemporary concept: 'Microlearning is a way of teaching and delivering content to learners in small, very specific bursts. The learners are in control of what and when they're learning' (Eades 2014). Some studies have indicated that when traditional sessions are broken into microlearning sessions, it improves retention and far transfer (Clark & Mayer 2011; Hug, Lindner & Bruck 2006; Hug 2015; van der Meer et al. 2015).

The analysis of *the TTP study* showed that chunking worked well when it was spaced over time: 'One of the challenges that we confronted and resolved was why we don't break down the eight-week course into what we call microlearning courses' [project leader]. The spaced shorter sessions allowed appropriate reflection and practice required to learn a complex skill. Some of the benefits mentioned by the project leaders were: delivers learning in short chunks, reduces the cognitive load of a complex skill, gives a sense of achievement, provides the time needed to practice the complex skill, allows an opportunity to reflect, to cite a few.

Such short chunked sessions have become necessary for e-learning modules as studies have shown that the attention spans of people have been reduced over the years, from 12 seconds in the year 2000 to 8 seconds in the year 2013 (Grovo 2014). These observations are supportive of other research studies. In a most recent study, van der Meer et al. (2015) reported that when a traditional lecture was replaced with bite-sized videos, over 45% of the students found learning useful and preferred this method. Lingg (2014) recommends that 'Rather than designing your next multi-hour course, consider creating several smaller 'learning snacks' instead' (p. 12). The short, quick, on-the-job instructor-facilitated sessions or short videos targeting one learning outcome at a time could effectively drive retention and absorption, and hence speed to proficiency.

The second part of this strategy really is spacing the chunked sessions in time, which provided the reinforcement or boost to the learners at regular intervals. This led to better retention of skill or knowledge being learned, similar to the observations noted by several researchers (Birnbaum et al. 2013). The shorter e-learning sessions spaced out in time are not only effective but also could be a strategy to accelerate speed to proficiency.

**Design guidelines**

- Teach and deliver content to learners in small, but specific bursts.
- Let learners be in control of what and when they are learning.
- Design short microlearning sessions per learning outcome.
- Determine appropriate spacing between two consecutive learning sessions.
- Sequence the microlearning sessions arranged as a learning path.

## 5.5    STRATEGY #3: SCENARIO-BASED CONTEXTUALIZATION OF E-LEARNING

Several studies suggested that learning must be contextualized for accelerated learning to happen. 'Contextualization' is to link the task at hand to the realist job environment and realistic challenges (Clark & Mayer 2013). Supporting those arguments, *the TTP study* findings showed that designing e-learning around real job challenges could accelerate proficiency in highly complex skills. Such methods enabled learners to solve real-world problems by triggering higher-order thinking as opposed to memorizing abstract concepts. 'If they apply that knowledge in the case [scenario], then they are more likely to remember because they are actively using their knowledge and secondly and most importantly, it's now tied to [the] context of use, so it's more likely to be remembered and applied later on at the workplace' [project leader].

Some method cited by the project leaders in *the TTP study* included *case-based curriculum, problem-based e-learning, scenario-based simulation, simulated scenarios, gaming or gamification, strategic rehearsal*, and variations thereof. Some of the plausible ways to build a context in e-learning were to drive learners to analyze a real-life scenario; solve the stated problem; describe the root cause; recommend a solution; make a decision, or explore an option, etc. This contextualization approach is highly supported and advocated by previous studies (Clark & Mayer 2013; Dror, Schmidt & O'connor 2011; Hinterberger 2011; Lesgold et al. 1988; Sitzmann 2010). Among past studies, Gott & Lesgold (2000) and Clark & Mayer (2013) established that various methods of real-life contextualization could accelerate the expertise of people.

Cases or scenarios provide a rich context for learning. This simple term 'scenario' refers to various variations of problem-based e-learning, case-based e-learning, gamification of scenarios, simulated cases, and virtual reality-based games. In previous studies on these lines, Clark & Mayer (2013) introduced that if e-learning is designed around scenarios, it enhances cognitively complex learning. Scenarios could be real cases or fabricated cases from real-life. The short or large scenarios employ the power of storytelling and bringing context in play. Arnold & Collier (2013) demonstrated that a sequence of cases through e-learning resulted in rapid expertise development of highly complex decision-making in novice-level financial professionals. Clark & Mayer (2013) advocated that scenario-based e-learning hold the potential to accelerate expertise. They emphasize the use and importance of scenarios:

By working through a series of job scenarios that could take months or years to complete in the work environment, the experience is compressed. In essence, scenario-based e-Learning is job experience in a box – designed to be unpackaged and stored in the learner's memory. Unlike real-world experience, scenario-based e-Learning scenarios not only compress time but also offer a sequence and structure of events designed to guide learning in a controlled manner. (Clark & Mayer 2013)

The emotional loading experienced by learners while solving real-life scenarios also helped in accelerating proficiency. Real-life scenarios appear to trigger emotional loading and involvement in learners due to immediate relevance to the job and the consequences thereof. It is noted from previous research studies that emotional involvement and loading plays a significant role in the effectiveness of online learning (Schuwirth 2013).

Scenarios also trigger active learning in which learners are fully involved. Clark & Mayer (2011) specified eight strategies to develop effective e-learning, the most important one in the context of complex learning being 'active processing' suggested by 11 studies they analyzed. They stated that 'People learn by actively processing information, which includes constructing mental models of learned information' (Clark & Mayer 2011, p. 65). Dror, Schmidt & O'connor (2011) supported the idea that e-learning could be used for acquisition of complex cognitive and hands-on skills such as used in the medical domain 'through challenging interactions that require the learners to take an active role in the training and learning experience' (Dror, Schmidt & O'connor 2011, p. 293). Another strategy, 'Problem-based curriculum' has shown evidence in triggering "active processing" in learners, a key component to accelerating complex skill acquisition (Clark & Mayer 2011). For example, Hinterberger (2011) used problem-based learning to teach computer science in "digital laboratory" settings in order to allow learners to acquire skills through the application of software in solving physical problems or phenomenon.

*The TTP study* noted that adding intentional or planned errors or bugs in the scenarios led to the active involvement of learners and triggered deeper thinking when teaching complex skills: 'That is letting students [to] struggle with something, try to solve something where their chances of succeeding are very low and then when they get instructions on the material, they more than make up that time in terms of how well and how permanently they learn' [project leader]. Thus, incorporating failures into learning added certain pressures and generated emotional involvement which in turn appeared to accelerate the speed toward proficiency. 'Those higher levels of emotional response are very, very key to embed[ing] the learning ... in fact, emotions play a huge role in how we learn' [project leader]. A similar observation was noted by DiBello, Missildine & Struttman (2009), Bjork (2013) and Clark & Mayer (2013) who confirmed that e-learning sessions designed using scenarios particularly by incorporating intentional failures might shorten the time to proficiency in the complex skill. The early studies by Gott & Lesgold (2000) in military settings showed that 25 hours of scenario-based simulation on the computer accelerated the expertise of 2 years technicians in diagnosing electrical faults in aircraft as equivalent to those holding 10 years of experience.

Gamification has emerged as one of the recent advances in e-learning strongly believed to build and accelerate the experience in complex skills which otherwise are hard to encounter in real-life or are not feasible to simulate or practice in real-life (Higgins 2015). For example, developing or accelerating skills of firefighters to fight with fire in a real fire incident or accelerating skills of underground miners to respond to emergency protocols in the event of the fire. Such situations may require higher-order complex cognitive skills like problem-solving, decision-making or troubleshooting (Slootmaker et al. 2014).

Use of computer-based simulated games (another form of e-learning) is one of the highly talked about e-learning strategy holding potential to accelerate proficiency. It has shown great potential in accelerating development of complex knowledge and skills in topics like cell biology, aviation, transportation, military and business management (Higgins 2015). In a research study, Sitzmann (2010) reported 20% higher confidence of learners after using computer-based simulation games, compared to classroom instruction which resulted in a higher transfer of knowledge and skills to the workplace. Dror, Schmidt & O'connor (2011, p. 293) advocated an approach of 'Technology Enhanced Learning' to facilitate the acquisition of complex cognitive and hands-on skills commonly used in the medical domain using technology to create challenging interactions. Dror, Schmidt & O'connor (2011, p. 294) highlighted the value of gaming as an e-learning strategy in complex skills training by stating that 'Another element in which gaming can be an efficient technological tool is in training how to cope with unexpected events.'

## Design guidelines

- Design e-learning by contextualizing, that is, linking the task to be taught to the realist job environment and realistic challenges one may face in that job.
- Use variations of scenario-based e-learning including problems, cases, games, virtual reality, simulation etc.
- Try several different ways to incorporate context: To analyze a real-life scenario; to solve the stated problem; to describe the root cause; to provide the recommendation on a solution; to make a decision; To choose between available options; to explore or extend an option.
- Allow a tangible sense of achievements while completing e-learning modules (like credits, points, scores).
- Put stakes in e-learning like consequences, failures, deliverables, reviews etc.

## 5.6  STRATEGY #4: ON-DEMAND ELECTRONIC PERFORMANCE SUPPORT SYSTEMS

Another theme observed in this study was that organizations deployed more electronic performance support systems (EPSS) in place of or in augmentation of training. EPSS included mostly the electronics resources like online learning content, reference material, knowledge-base, procedures, mobile applications, decision-making software, etc. which according to the project leaders can provide just-in-time training or just-in-time support. Raybould (1995) view all computer-based training, knowledge assets, information sources as a subset of EPSS, rather than as an alternative approach. It is also imperative to say here that with the availability of new technologies, the shape and extent of PSS are also changing beyond its original role of just-in-time resource for training or support or information. 'Organizational learning moves from being a training event to which employees need to be invited, to something that happens automatically as employees seek assistance on-the-job from EPSS' [project leader].

Most of the designers in *the TTP study* suggested taking the content out from instructor-led sessions and making it accessible through EPSS as self-paced learning activities to prepare the learners. 'We will take the [informational] content out .. and we'll make it available so that people have access to that before they come to a course' [project leader]. By doing so, employees accessed the resources at their own pace, rather than at the pace of the instructor, which significantly cut the time from proficiency cycle. This not only made good use of the learner's time while waiting for the instructor-led session, but it also allowed the formal training intervention to focus more on critical and complex hands-on skills.

If strategically deployed, performance systems could either augment or completely replace the training interventions. Arnold &

Collier (2013) demonstrated that an e-learning system designed around an expert system and case-based e-learning accelerated the expertise of new financial analysts, providing highly complex decision-making to business corporations without actually requiring any training. It is also noticed that EPSS can be used as part of the formal class or training itself can be delivered via EPSS itself: 'By integrating the learning material (such as scenario-based questions) into the business procedures, the EPSS becomes a powerful online learning platform. By tracking employee progress through the procedure-based exercises they need to complete in order to achieve and prove competence, the EPSS can integrate with a Learning Management System (LMS) to provide a comprehensive map of organization learning and competence achievement' [project leader].

Another finding of this research indicated that learners gained proficiency in content faster when they used or accessed content based on the need of the task at hand, rather than learning it beforehand. So a conscious effort to remove unnecessary informational content from the training modules led to shorter training time. This corroborated with Gery (1991) who advocates using EPSSs to provide individualized online access instead of the information content-heavy training upfront. By using PSS to deliver informational content, the formal training intervention can focus more on critical human skills required for proficiency. One reason PSS could accelerate proficiency is its ability to reinforce learning and knowledge at specified intervals.

While there is plenty of literature and research on EPSS, *the TTP study* provides grounds that when proficiency goals are viewed holistically, several non-training resources such as performance support systems need to be used in conjunction with training-focused events. Such complementation allows a learner to attain proficiency in several complex skills in a shorter time.

## 5.7   STRATEGY #5: OPTIMALLY SEQUENCED E-LEARNING PATH

Data analysis revealed that time to proficiency is significantly impacted by carefully sequencing the learning activities, tasks or assignments in a very efficient path, called 'learning path' or 'learning pathway.' The concept of learning path is to eliminate redundant, irrelevant or wasteful activities in learning path by selecting most essential and relevant learning activities (e-learning or otherwise) required for a stated proficiency goal, and then sequencing those through readily available resources (e-learning modules or otherwise) to achieve that goal in shortest possible time. The essence of the strategy is 'if you sequence those activities [....] over a period of time, you can pull together a whole sequence of activities and in effect what you're doing is not waiting for the universe to provide them' [project leader].

In the context of e-learning, activities included online courses, use of electronic resources, practice on PSS, other knowledge tools and a range of other e-learning activities which when sequenced optimally is termed as e-learning path.

The learning sequence suggested in this study is not the same as what the most academic literature portrays, that is, individualized or personalized learning path of a learner in reference to learning the material rather than gaining the proficiency. Rosenbaum & Williams (2004) demonstrated the use of the learning path concept in many commercial settings. By approaching the sequence from a learner's proficiency angle, a designer could map available e-learning resources in a path in an optimal order of activities that shorten the time to proficiency, as suggested in figure 11.

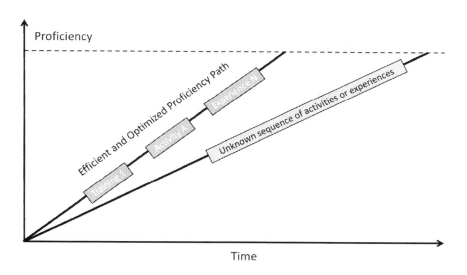

*Figure 11: Concept of an optimal path (Image inspired from Steve Rosenbaum, Learning Paths International 2010, learningatlightspeed.wordpress.com)*

The project leaders said that 'if you can set up a way, a very systematic set of cases, a systematic set of experiences and organize those [cases] then you could speed up that process [of proficiency acquisition] because you need to have those experiences' [project leader].

Further, by assigning time targets to each activity including online and e-learning activities the total time to proficiency could be estimated and tracked and then focused efforts could be made to shorten the time. The sequencing was made optimal by using some criteria like frequency of occurrence of the task (very frequent to rare), usage of the knowledge or skill (very often to hardly), the complexity of the task (simple to complex) and difficulty level of the problem (very simple to very hard). It is also found that when business criteria such as frequency, complexity, or difficulty of the task were used to sequence the e-learning modules, resources, activities and microlearning sessions, the result was an efficient and lean learning path. This efficient learning path then contributed significantly toward the goal of attaining proficiency faster.

Such sequencing in a 'learning path' played a pivotal role to reduce the time the learner takes to reach targeted proficiency (Attri & Wu 2015). Previously, in the context of the complex jobs, Darrah (1996) showed the use of a sequence of organized activities in a computer manufacturing company while Hutchins & Palen (1997) explain it for a flight engineer's role. This was seen as an influential strategy for accelerated proficiency.

In some cases, when the learners were provided with a head-start based on their prior learning, current skill assessment, and other experience; it could accelerate time to proficiency. This involved conducting systematic profiling of learners needs which can then be used to build an adaptive learning path to shorten the journey to proficiency collectively. A classic example of this strategy is Pearson Education's MyITlab online e-learning system which performs an initial assessment on the learner and allows different 'adaptive' entry and exit points depending on current skills, knowledge or experience [http://myitlabvh.pearsoncmg.com/learn-about/adaptive-learning.html]. It also conducts continuous assessment tied to learning outcomes and based on results, dynamically select activities or modules in the learning path.

**Design guidelines**

- Eliminate redundant, irrelevant or wasteful activities in the learning path. Select the most essential and relevant learning activities (e-learning or otherwise) required for a stated proficiency goal.
- Sequence those through readily available resources and avenues in natural settings to achieve that goal in the shortest possible time.

- Approach from business goals – not like individualized or personalized learning path.
- Map the learning activities vs. available opportunities and focus on the optimal order.
- Profile learners on their prior learning, current skill assessment, and other experience. Design a learning path which allows different 'adaptive' entry and exit points based on the learner's profile which gives a head-start to learners.
- Conduct a continuous assessment of learning outcomes, and dynamically select activities or modules in the learning path to collectively shorten the journey to proficiency.

## 5.8   SUMMARY OF RECOMMENDATIONS

The model discussed in this chapter is in fact pretty simple. It is recommended that designers perform an overall comprehensive analysis of the learning outcomes first. A detailed matrix of learning outcomes (what to learn), delivery methods (how to deliver) and delivery modes (when to deliver) should be prepared for design decisions. Such a matrix or blueprint of learning outcomes allows designers to assess which of the learning outcomes should be delivered using e-learning and which learning outcomes can be attained only in the classroom settings. This blueprint also allows designers to decide what can be learned by the learners before formal classroom training and what makes the best sense to learn alongside the task in the actual job.

Each learning outcome can be designed as small chunks of content or a microlearning session. These sessions should be distributed in time with appropriate spacing. The sessions can then be sequenced in the form of an e-learning path to help learners progress in their proficiency in quick short steps. Designers may be able to insert various self-paced and instructor-led sessions at the most appropriate points in the path based on complexity and difficulty levels of the learning outcomes. For example, if topic demands attention, reflection and deeper thinking to prepare for the next ILT session, then corresponding pre-work can be inserted as self-paced homework activities on the e-learning path between the consecutive ILT sessions.

The attempt should be made to design each microlearning session around scenarios and problems. The scenario-based short sessions can be delivered through EPSSs which include a range of tools like LMS, learning on the go, mobile learning, and decision support systems. As an example, Arnold & Collier (2013) demonstrated the use of an expert system in which an extensive database of pre-design financial analysis cases was loaded. The cases were profiled based on complexity and skill levels and other subject matter. These cases were then sequenced based on the blueprints of learning outcomes targeted for the job of financial analysts. The cases were presented to learners on their devices in a suitable progression of complexity, which guided them to reach the desired proficiency goal in a shorter time. On similar lines, for disciplines such as medical, engineering and business studies, each chunked blended e-learning session could very well be designed around a case or a scenario to build the context in learning. Some of the plausible ways to build the context in e-learning modules are by engaging learners to analyze a real-life scenario, solve a problem, investigate the root cause; answer situational questions; explore different options, recommend solutions and assess a strategy for real-world implementation. Such methods of contextualization will actively involve the learners and will trigger deeper thinking in them.

Furthermore, in some disciplines like clinical, equipment maintenance, electronics, software, and aviation, it is possible to design a curriculum with a simulation of intentional errors, bugs, and failures, to drive deeper thinking in learners. During these activities, whether self-paced or instructor-led, learners are engaged actively in tasks such as computing, processing, transforming etc. as opposed to just reading the content.

To implement these strategies, there are several different methods, technologies, and tools available (Attri & Wu 2015). A detailed list of methods was presented at the Elearning Forum Asia Conference[5] as a paper titled *"E-Learning Strategies to Accelerate Time-to-Proficiency in Acquiring Complex Skills"* (Attri & Wu 2015). Author's general belief is that the effectiveness of these strategies can be further enhanced with the use of the latest e-learning technologies, mobile applications, content delivery platforms, and other collaboration systems.

[5] Attri, R. K. & Wu, W. S. (2015). E-Learning Strategies to Accelerate Time-to-Proficiency in Acquiring Complex Skills: Preliminary Findings. Paper presented at *E-learning Forum Asia Conference*, Jun 2015. Singapore: SIM University, available at <https://www.researchgate.net/publication/282647943>.

# CHAPTER 6

# FIVE INSTRUCTIONAL STRATEGIES TO ACCELERATE PROFICIENCY[6]

One of the key things that stood out in *the TTP study* is that ILT phase, if managed well, could impact the initial head-start of an individual if s/he is unfamiliar to the assigned job. In fact, the role of training toward accelerating proficiency is well-accepted. 'We also believe that reducing Time to Proficiency is the most significant contribution the training function can deliver to the organization' (Rosenbaum & Williams 2004, p. 14). New and more efficient, more effective instructional strategies are required that can bring employees up to speed quickly.

---

[6] A version of this chapter was presented in a conference: Attri, RK & Wu, WS 2016, "Classroom-based instructional strategies to accelerate proficiency of employees in complex job skills," paper presented to the Asian American Conference for Education, Singapore, 15-16 January, available at <https://www.researchgate.net/publication/303803099>.

This chapter intends to describe early-stage findings of *the TTP study* that revealed five instructional strategies that were successfully applied by organizations to accelerate time to proficiency in complex job skills.

## 6.1 ROLE OF CLASSROOM TRAINING TO ACCELERATE PROFICIENCY

Day in and day out employees are expected to handle complex problems and derive solutions to achieve remedies to these complex problems. In the process of solving, they experience a high level of emotional loading due to pressures, timelines, stresses, speed, expectations and other factors. However, ironically, organizations tend to copy "an academic educational" model of classroom training in their work settings. For instance, a complex job of a site safety professional may end up getting delivered inside the closed walls of a classroom with a project and with a curriculum which is content-heavy, but context-light.

Further, such classroom training pulls the people out of their jobs (i.e., context) where there is a "safe" environment with unrealistically low loading on emotions and mind. Further, such classroom training sessions tend to be instructor-centric, and follows a rigid institutionalized structure. While there are several new techniques like problem-based learning and others like flipped classroom type of concepts, the classroom training solutions stay largely one-size-fits-all.

Such training sessions tend to have too much content just because employees are being taught "just in case" content to prepare them to handle some event, without having a full realistic understanding of how often such an event happens. Due to inherent inertia in even developing such training sessions, the overall time to proficiency of employees is very long. Thus, conventional classroom instructional strategies do not work when the goal is to speed up the proficiency curve of employees.

Several researchers have voiced and argued about the value of formal instructor-led training or classroom training particular in low-frequency tasks and rare events. Another place classroom training is a compelling option is when training involves highly complex skills. Complex job skills refer to higher-order skills such as problem-solving, troubleshooting, critical thinking, complex technical and personal interactions and higher-order decision-making. Acquisition of proficiency in complex skill is a slow process. However, business still requires a faster speed to proficiency in complex skills. That requires more effective classroom or instructional strategies to reduce time to proficiency of employees.

Though the research on training and learning has come up with several different techniques, it has lacked a practical solution for corporate settings to accelerate the proficiency of employees in a shorter time. *The TTP study* revealed five strategies for classroom or instructor-led instructions that were seen to hold great potential in accelerating proficiency of employees. These strategies were presented at the American Asian Conference at Singapore in a paper titled *"Classroom-Based Instructional Strategies to Accelerate Proficiency of Employees in Complex Job Skills"* (Attri & Wu 2016).

The model of five instructional strategies is described in the sections that follow.

## 6.2 CONCEPTUAL MODEL OF INSTRUCTIONAL STRATEGIES

During preliminary phases of the research study, a conceptual model was developed to see how five instructional strategies interplay to accelerate speed to proficiency. The model is shown in figure 12 superimposed on phases of training and proficiency growth (discussed in Chapter 3). The horizontal axis is time, and the vertical axis is the hypothetical proficiency levels from P0 to P5. P0 represents the proficiency of someone in a given role at the outset. P3 represents the desired or target proficiency defined for a role.

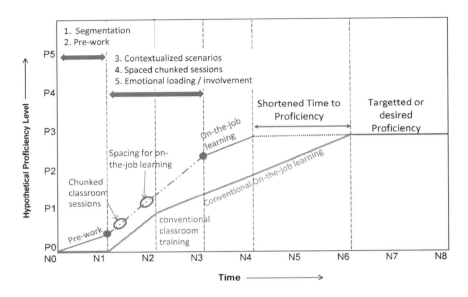

*Figure 12: Proficiency growth and instructional strategies to shorten time to proficiency (Copyrights Raman K. Attri)*

The solid line in figure 12 shows the traditional learning curve represented as simplified straight lines in a piece-wise manner. Typically during time N0 to N1, a learner may be just waiting for classroom training if the job is technically intensive and required new knowledge/skills to perform the job. Several jobs do offer some block of time for classroom-based training, focused on a product or process or service. Traditional training is typically classroom-based and instructor-centric, which are denoted as 'traditional ILT' curve in a simple piece-wise representation, leading the learner to proficiency level P1. Once this training is over at time N2, typically remaining tasks and skills are learned on-the-job through several assignments, projects, and tasks. Assuming piece-wise representation in simplistic terms, the 'traditional on-the-job learning' curve would lead the learner to attain desired proficiency eventually in time N6.

The findings of this study suggested an accelerated path to proficiency through five classroom instructional strategies. The proficiency growth curve can be altered and can be accelerated using these strategies so that the learners attain desired proficiency in time N4, as shown with simplified piece-wise straight lines. The mechanism of accelerating proficiency path is as follows:

As a first strategy, it is found that segmentation of critical tasks is extremely critical which allows deciding what skills learners can learn before they come to formal classroom training, what should be learned during the classroom and what should be learned during the on-the-job learning phase. This is an exercise that needs to happen at time N0 well before a learner comes onboard.

Between N0 to N1 time, while learners are waiting for formal classroom training, providing self-guided pre-work and learning assignments to the learners allows them to learn at their pace. By the time learners are ready to go into a formal classroom session, they would have gained some proficiency, though not very high, in certain skills or knowledge. The key activities, content, and knowledge are identified as pre-work, usually done as self-guided learning, may conceptually allow uplifting the initial entry-level proficiency slightly with which a learner starts the classroom training. This accelerated approach in this phase is shown as 'pre-work curve' between time N0 to N1.

The classroom training is made longer between N1 to N3. Now the classrooms are not a single event or a contiguous block of time. Three strategies are implemented concurrently during the classroom training sessions. Inside the classroom training, instead of a contiguous block of time for instructions, it is seen that classroom sessions were chunked appropriately and delivered in shorter meaningful sessions. The key strategy to design these sessions is contextualization with scenarios. Each session is designed around scenarios or problems, and each session attempts to provide a measurable ability to handle or solve certain kinds of problems or situations one is likely to encounter at the job.

Another strategy seen effective alongside scenario-based contextualization is to space these sessions in time. The spacing works best when consecutive sessions were interleaved with on-the-job activities, tasks or assignments. The benefit of this approach is that a learner was actually involved in doing job assignments based on what s/he learned in the chunked sessions.

The last strategy seen in *the TTP study* analysis is to use realistic job tasks which learners were required to deliver. Such real jobs would build the emotional loading of time pressure, quality expectations associated with the deliverable, and general dynamics of the job midst of which one is required to deliver.

Though each strategy in itself could be successful in isolation, however, time to proficiency appears to be impacted hugely if all five strategies are orchestrated together in the appropriate mix based on context, job roles, and business challenges. Doing all the above together could result in a higher level of proficiency that is attained out of such training compared to traditional training. While the length of the formal classroom training may increase from original time N2 to N3 due to time-spacing and interleaving, the resultant proficiency ends up much higher than proficiency P1 otherwise attained in a traditional classroom training.

The rate of acceleration depends on how well sessions are chunked, skills delivered in those chunked sessions, and the spacing between two chunked sessions. It also depends on the quality of on-the-job assignments interleaved between two chunked sessions and the level of emotional loading/ involvement.

In some settings, such an arrangement of 'chunked time-spaced sessions interleaved with on-the-job learning' might continue till learners reach desired proficiency in terms of delivering on-the-job performance. However, in other settings, it may be pure on-the-job learning that continues from N3 to N4. Learners may seek support from peers, PSS and other tools or just-in-time learning as and when needed during on-the-job learning. Conceptually, the learners would have a great head-start advantage during on-the-job learning. As a result, learners are likely to attain desired proficiency in time N4 instead of time N6 which otherwise would have been required using the traditional approach.

## 6.3    STRATEGY #1: SEGMENTATION OF CRITICAL TASKS

'Classroom is a place to learn the skills which cannot be learned in any other mode' [project leader].

The research findings suggested that the mastery of all skills or knowledge was not required to produce a given outcome, or at least was not required to be learned upfront. Also, not all skills included in a training program were so equally frequent, critical or essential for a given job that acquiring all of them at once was required. Thus, it was suggested that the technique to segment and categorize tasks, skills, events, activities, etc., be used, based on characteristics such as frequency, complexity, criticality and the nature of skills through data analytics. Experts found it beneficial to focus on two things: first, the things that mattered the most at the job toward producing desired outcomes; and second, the most frequent events (i.e., tasks, skills or tools) that a performer was inevitably going to encounter at his job. Segmentation prioritized what was essential. This strategy also determined how a given skill should be delivered depending on criticality and nature of category – it could be self-guided material or it could be a hands-on session.

**Design Guidelines**

- Segment the tasks by criticality, importance, frequency, and impact.
- Cover the most critical tasks which cannot be learned in self-guided mode or on-the-job or any other modes.
- Focus on the job rather than the training or content.
- Focus classroom training on human and behavioral skills.
- Take the content out and make it self-guided.

## 6.4 STRATEGY #2: SELF-GUIDED PRE-WORK/ PREPARATION

'Preparing learners on certain learning outcomes before the instructor-led session cuts the training time' [project leader].

Pre-work helped to develop a thorough 'prior understanding' required for next instructor-led sessions and it utilized learner's wait time before an instructor-led session. The project leaders highlighted pre-work strategy as 'model begins with a preparation phase, so you would prepare the learners to learn, to come to the workshop, but you may give them work to do beforehand' [project leader]. Tullis & Benjamin (2011) and de Jonge et al. (2015) demonstrated that by providing self-paced self-study content to learners, memory and recall performance could improve.

The project leaders suggested making content self-paced and accessible before instructor-led sessions, 'we will take the [information] content out … and we'll make it available so that people have access to that before they come to a course' [project leader]. The project leaders reported using blended microlearning sessions to provide content for the learner's self-study prior to instructor-led sessions.

Several project leaders emphasized the importance of leveraging 'prior understanding' of the learners in order to accelerate the learning. The project leaders mentioned that 'They will also make use of what people have actually learned from the past and actually use those experiences to build on what they already know. ... If you can build on what people already know then you're not starting from scratch, [not] starting from a brand new concept' [project leader]. The prior learning, if leveraged well, provided learners a head-start for instructor-led sessions and hence could accelerate the learning.

However, a self-paced content study in itself was not sufficient. Responses from interviews suggested that pre-work led to accelerated learning only when it was designed around specific learning outcomes. Further, a deep understanding of content was build through appropriately designed pre-work or assignments which drive learners to think deeper.

This study argued that by making the content available to learners along with well-designed pre-work, face-to-face learning becomes more effective. One of the approaches could be to design low complexity skills including informational content as a pre-training course to give head-start to learners. Then, self-guided homework assignments are designed to cover medium complex skills which require deeper thinking and reflection. Such reflective practices are considered to accelerate skill transfer. Subsequently, highly complex skills are covered during ILT sessions. It appeared that leveraging pre-work and homework strategically to supplement ILT sessions during the pre-training and ILT phase could accelerate time to proficiency. Notably, a well-managed pre-training phase is instrumental in lifting up the entry-level proficiency of learners into the formal ILT sessions.

**Design Guidelines**

- Design well-defined pre-ILT pre-work to deliver specific learning outcomes.
- Focus on covering low complexity skills including informational content in the pre-ILT pre-work.
- Design self-guided homework assignments between distributed ILT sessions.
- Focus on medium complex skills requiring deeper thinking in homework assignments that allow space, time and opportunity for reflection before the next day's ILT session.
- Focus on highly complex skills during ILT or classroom training sessions.
- Leverage prior understanding of the learners.
- Drive reflection and deeper thinking.

## 6.5   STRATEGY #3: CONTEXTUALIZE LEARNING WITH SCENARIOS

'Time-to-proficiency gets accelerated if learning happens in the context of the actual job or learning is contextualized' [project leader].

Higher-order complex cognitive skills are typically non-linear in nature, that is, the problem space and approaches could be fuzzy and structured rules may not be applicable all the time. Hence one-way static e-learning may not work effectively. Several studies emphasize active participation as a key to accelerating learning in complex skill acquisition. The studies have emphasized different elements of this strategies viz. learning by doing, learning through active processing and learning through active participation, non-linear thinking and decision-making etc. (Clark & Mayer 2011; Dror, Schmidt & O'connor 2011).

Study findings show a large number of evidence that designing learning around real job challenges accelerates learning of highly complex skills. The project leaders mentioned that 'We try to identify what are the common cases or scenario in the field that happened to that [are related to training] module. ... so we create a similar scenario at the beginning of the module training' [project leader]. In literature, such an approach is termed 'contextualization', which refers to linking the task at hand to the real job environment and realistic challenges (Clark & Mayer 2013; Dror, Schmidt & O'connor 2011; Hinterberger 2011; Lesgold et al. 1988; Sitzmann 2010). Contextualized scenario-based learning strategy in various forms is basically a problem-solving process which drives learner's active involvement in the learning and triggers the deeper non-linear thinking as well.

Several problem-based methods were used by experts to design learning with contexts such as case-based curriculum, case-based expert system, problem-based learning, scenario-based simulation, simulated scenarios, gaming or gamification, strategic rehearsal, and variations thereof. These methods make students to solve real-world problems as opposed to memorizing abstract concepts[7]. 'We could see that rich cases had a very distinct advantage in some scenarios' [project leader]. Such problem-based contextualized learning methods triggered deeper thinking among learners, 'So the training is broken into stages, where we give them some knowledge and then we will call back to the case [scenario] again where we start to ask them to think, to apply the knowledge to solve the problem' [project leader]. The obstacles, problems, desirable failures and mistakes built into learning

---

[7] Interested reader may refer to detailed guidelines on problem-centric instructions design in this book - Attri, RK 2018, *5 Problem-Centered Design Methods and 6 Design Strategies for Training Real-World Problem-Solving Skills,* Ebook ISBN 9789811188916, Speed To Proficiency Research: S2Pro©, Singapore, available as Kindle book in Amazon and for download at <http://www.lulu.com/shop/ebook/product-23882226.html>.

curriculum has long proven its potential to deepen the learning and accelerate skill acquisition by Bjork & Linn (2006), DiBello, Missildine & Struttman (2009) and Bjork (2013). By incorporating intentional mistakes, failures, and errors in the curriculum, deeper thinking is triggered which compensates for any slowdown by actually accelerating learning: 'they more than make up that time in terms of how well and how permanently they learn' [project leader].

Contextual learning allowed learners to get involved actively in the learning process. 'Once you adopt a training model where you take people away from the context of the workplace, you actually limit the ceiling' [project leader]. Active learning means that learners are learning by doing, actively processing information and both mind and body are engaged in learning activities (Silberman & Auerbach, 2006). Active involvement through 'learning by doing' is evident from this comment: 'The activities that you design will be around exploring some of the concepts, so there has to be a model of some sort. And you might layout the model, you might get them to play with it in some way, but get them to interact with that and give their thoughts about it, try and get them to relate' [project leader]. Active learning through thinking and active processing is suggested as: 'So what we want is for the [learners] to start thinking. What is this error message about? What is this problem about? And then from there, they start to figure out what they need to learn in order to really troubleshoot and solve the problem' [project leader]. Role of such active involvement in accelerating the learning is recognized by Clark and Mayer (2011) as 'people learn by actively processing information' (p.65). Several other studies also supported the fact that active involvement of learners is an important factor that accelerates learning, proficiency, and expertise (Clark & Mayer 2013; Dror, Schmidt & O'connor 2011; Fadde & Klein 2012; Hinterberger 2011; Klein, Hintze & Saab 2013; Phillips, Klein & Sieck 2004). There is some compelling evidence from research that active involvement and non-linear thinking strategy accelerates proficiency in traditional face-to-face settings (Fadde & Klein 2012; Hinterberger 2011; Klein, Hintze & Saab 2013; Phillips, Klein & Sieck 2004). This appears to apply to e-learning settings too.

*The TTP study* findings indicated that contextual experiences, in a training intervention or at the job, contributed toward accelerating proficiency when performers were actively immersed in the task with similar challenges they encountered at the workplace.

**Design Guidelines**

- Use real-world and real-world context in the classroom.
- Design a variety of real-world scenarios, actual cases, simulations and role-plays.
- 'Gamify' the situations as real as possible.
- Leverage real-life work events instead of a content-focused training strategy.
- Increase active participation by incorporating interactivity and encouraging learning by doing.
- Trigger non-linear thinking process in learners by using higher-order scenarios, real-life cases, and job-relevant assessment.
- Ask learners to generate some deliverables, compute something, process information, and transform content.
- Use thinking based assessment, that is, questions that require some kind of research, active involvement, and deeper thinking.

## 6.6 STRATEGY #4: EMOTIONAL LOADING/ EMOTIONAL INVOLVEMENT

'Workplace challenges and consequences drive the emotional loading of an individual in a task, e.g. aggressive timelines, consequences of errors, complex interactions which impact speed to proficiency' [project leader].

As opposed to the traditional approach of keeping emotions out of training, experts incorporated emotions and emotional loading similar to what a real workplace challenge would drive. That included similar pressures, stakes, consequences, time constraints, performance specifications and team dynamics to what would occur while doing the task in the real job. Preliminary findings suggest that same kind of emotional involvement, emotional stakes or reactions in the learning sense of 'what is on the line' to accelerate time to proficiency. Far transfer and time to proficiency appear to have some link with emotional involvement and stakes during learning: 'emotions play a huge role in how we learn' [project leader]. An example of triggering emotions in learning is by adding time pressure, whereby 'users are required to move to the next task at some predetermined time interval, inducing a potential time pressure' [project leader]. It appears from the finding that by incorporating emotions and emotional involvement, learning can be accelerated as good as on-the-job learning. Several researchers have recognized emotions, emotional reactions and emotional involvement as important ingredients for the success of learning (Dirkx 2001; Kort, Reilly & Picard 2001; Shen, Wang & Shen 2009; Värlander 2008). Most recently Trigwell, Ellis & Han (2012) and Schuwirth (2013) demonstrated some positive relationship between emotions and learning effectiveness.

The findings in this study also indicate that incorporating failures into learning add certain pressures and generate an emotional involvement which in turn appear to accelerates learning. In addition to triggering deep thinking, correctly designed failures, simulated errors, pressures, and real-life context also trigger emotional reactions in learners. Various studies provide some guidance on adding desirable errors (Bjork & Linn 2006; Bjork 2013) and rapid failure cycles in a compressed time (DiBello, Missildine & Struttman 2009) which not only keep learners emotionally involved but also add stakes in the learning by integrating time pressure.

Today's workplace challenges and consequences of quality of a task, drive emotions in each task assigned to an individual because there are stakes involved in doing each task. To accelerate learning in the context of realities, training designers should design assignments around scenarios or other contextualized methods which introduce a reasonable and realistic level of pressure in the learning environment in terms of time, target, quality, and deliverables. For example, if the learning outcome of a given e-learning module is to 'create a sound business proposal', then it could be run as role play. Students may be assigned roles like functional heads or customers who would be required to evaluate a business proposal submitted by another student as an applicant. The applicant would need to defend his proposal to the questions raised by functional heads. Such an assignment will bring realistic pressure and trigger emotions and emotional involvement with the content. If emotional involvement and stakes are designed properly in the classroom learning using strategies of contextualization, it could lead to an acceleration in time to proficiency.

**Design Guidelines**

- Drive learning with stakes and a high degree of emotional involvement rather than always designing for 'a safe place to learn.'
- Promote learners' emotional involvement, emotional reactions to stakes in learning, and a sense of 'what is on the line.'
- Drive learning goals or outcomes closely or directly linked to on-the-job success or failure.
- Design realistic learning with a high degree of emotional loading rather than emphasizing 'a safe place to learn.'

- Add stakes and consequences of assigned tasks (what is on the line).
- Introduce the pressure of quality and timeline with peer review of the deliverables.

## 6.7 STRATEGY #5: SPACED DISTRIBUTED CHUNKED INTERVENTIONS

'Spacing the shorter sessions in time reinforces the retention of skills and proficiency' [project leader].

This finding is discussed in Chapter 4 in the context of strategy #2 'Time-spaced microlearning content' and inferences drawn there are equally applicable to classroom instructional design.

The findings suggested converting larger tasks or activities and lessons into smaller chunks, distributed over a period of time, delivered using PSS, technology or just-in-time systems. These small segments of learning are used just-in-time during other contextual activities such as job shadow. The findings suggested embedding learning and work together by interweaving training sessions and work assignments, which could allow authentic learning through on-the-job practice. The delivery of learning (chunked learning sessions) is kept closer to the point of need, and in the context of the job to accelerate proficiency. Performers should be made to work on things that were essential to producing outcomes.

**Design Guidelines**

- Split long classroom training into short learning activities.
- Design each chunked session around specific learning outcomes.
- Instead of a block of time, space and distribute the sessions.
- Provide opportunities for reflection and practice between sessions.

## 6.8    SUMMARY OF RECOMMENDATIONS

Classroom-based instructional strategies need to be rethought 'beyond classrooms' and 'beyond instructors' with real context and real job challenges using the following strategies:

- Segment and analyze criticality of skills
- Contextualize classroom training with scenarios, cases, simulations and live job activities
- Prepare learner with pre-work
- Space and distribute chunked learning sessions
- Create an emotional involvement and emotional loading

At the same time, it must be understood that classroom training is not the major source of accelerating proficiency. What it does is provide initial proficiency at an accelerated rate, particularly when skills involved are new, complex and requires hands-on practice in a controlled environment.

# CHAPTER 7

# THREE WORKPLACE LEARNING DESIGN STRATEGIES TO ACCELERATE PROFICIENCY[8]

The preliminary findings from *the TTP study* generated three workplace learning strategies and a conceptual framework that holds the potential to accelerate the proficiency of employees. It was seen that these three workplace learning strategies were invariably present in all the 66 project cases analyzed in *the TTP study*. These findings were presented at International Conference on Researching Work and Learning at Singapore, titled *"Conceptual Model of Workplace Training and Learning Strategies to Shorten Time-To-Proficiency in Complex Skills: Preliminary Findings"* (Attri & Wu 2015). This chapter describes the three workplace

---

[8] A version of this chapter was presented at a conference: Attri, RK & Wu, W 2015, 'Conceptual model of workplace training and learning strategies to shorten time-to-proficiency in complex skills: preliminary findings', paper presented to the 9th International Conference on Researching in Work and Learning (RWL), Singapore, 9-11 December, available at <https://www.researchgate.net/publication/286623558>.

learning strategies and the preliminary conceptual model. The chapter will describe how workplace learning and training interventions at the workplace are leveraged to shorten time to proficiency of employees.

## 7.1    ROLE OF WORKPLACE LEARNING TO ACCELERATE PROFICIENCY

The literature review of past studies has indicated quite a few workplace training strategies that may hold the potential to reduce time to proficiency. However, what is lacking is an integrated framework of strategies that could be scaled to different contexts, content and job roles. Hoffman, Feltovich, et al. (2010, p. 59) believe that 'there is relatively little research on training at the high end of the proficiency.'

According to Dreyfus & Dreyfus (1986), a proficient person uses intuition based on enough past experiences to solve new, unfamiliar and complex problems. This experience comes through one of three ways 1) while working on on-the-job assignments and tasks or 2) through a training curriculum which is designed to incorporate that experience (examples are problem-based learning, case-based training etc.) or 3) if training is embedded right into the workplace in the existing workflow. It is now believed that professionals develop and accelerate most of their proficiency while working and practicing at their jobs (Billett 1996; Eraut 2007).

Researchers have recognized that training should be extended to the work setting. Hoffman et al. (2009, p. 20) state that 'The modes and means of training should engage real work practice – the job challenges, context, and duties to the greatest extent possible.' Grossman et al. (2013, p. 315) also appealed that 'Beyond the formal training settings, another important area in need of future research is how training opportunities can be extended into the work environment.' Therefore, as opposed to formal training events, organizations should investigate more on workplace learning and on-the-job learning strategies to accelerate time to proficiency.

However, extending training into workplace settings has its challenges. According to Sheckley & Keeton (1999), individuals develop proficiency by working in challenging and supportive environments, self-monitoring, engaging in deliberate practice, and solving ill-defined problems. This learning experience is typically much unstructured and could be ad hoc at times. Rosenbaum & Williams (2004) noted that 70% to 80% of learning happens on-the-job through several unstructured activities that hamper the effective use of an employee's potential. Therefore, the real question is how to accelerate experience and proficiency in the workplace despite the random nature of workplace situations.

Despite challenges, workplace training and learning is gaining momentum as a mechanism to accelerate proficiency though it is still at infant stages. There are very few research studies available to support accelerated proficiency goals particularly in the acquisition of complex skills. Among traditional workplace training strategies, Structured OJT has reported a reduction in training durations in the low to medium complexity task environment (Jacobs & Bu-Rahmah 2012; Jacobs 2003, 2014). In their pioneer research compilation on *accelerated proficiency* (Hoffman, Feltovich, et al. 2010) and *accelerated expertise* (Hoffman et al. 2014), researchers enumerated several strategies for accelerating proficiency and expertise through training which include: computer games, simulation and immersion; case-based instructions with desirable difficulties (see Bjork & Bjork 2011); appropriately timed meaningful corrective feedback; compressing library of tough cases in a short time (see Hoffman et al. 2008); decision-making exercises (see Klein 2003) and operational simulations (see DiBello, Missildine & Struttman 2009). On a closer look, this is a mixture of instructor-led, as well as workplace-based training interventions.

Most of these methods are whole-task method, in which a particular task is taught as a whole (van Merriënboer, Clark & de Croock 2002). However, Fadde (2009a) proposes that complex skills like intuitive decision-making can be broken into sub-skills or sub-tasks such as detection, categorization, and prediction; and then one can develop targeted instructional design activities in workplace settings to accelerate those sub-skills (Fadde 2009b, 2009c, 2010, 2012).

Fadde & Klein (2012) state that one needs to practice expertise-oriented knowledge and skills through learning opportunities while doing his job. Ericsson et al. (1993) found that only practice that can accelerate expertise is highly focused and mentored 'Deliberate Practice' and that one needs minimum 10 years of such practice to achieve professional 'world-class' expertise. However, this theory is applicable in relatively closed and repetitive domains in which standards of measurements are well-defined, and outcomes are finite such as sports and music. In business domains, Fadde & Klein (2010) argue that professionals do not have that much time for deliberate practice on a narrow skill set in natural settings besides their roles. To address this, Fadde & Klein (2010, 2012) proposed a framework called 'deliberate performance,' also called Action Learning Activities (ALA), which leverages characteristics of day-to-day job like repetition of everyday routine work, timely feedback by superiors, task variety of the workplace, progressive difficulty of situations to accelerate expertise in domain-specific tacit knowledge and intuitive expertise.

Similar to the above, immersive strategies also showed promise in accelerating proficiency at the workplace. Such strategies include simulation, game-based learning, tabletop exercises, interactive stories, board games, and alternate reality games. As an example of immersive learning, Klein (2003) proposed 'decision-making exercises'

(DMXs) to accelerate complex decision-making at the workplace without taking the professionals out of their job. In the business context, Backus et al. (2010) put forth support for immersive learning as a way to accelerate leadership skills by stating that 'Immersive learning allows individuals to actively engage in real-world scenarios and make decisions that result in real-time consequences' (p. 145). Extending it further, Grossman et al. (2013) specified that decision-making expertise at work could be accelerated using some workplace training strategies such as simulation-based training, situational awareness, metacognition training, mental rehearsal, coaching and mentoring, motivation enhancement. They also indicate that '...many questions remain regarding the types and combinations of interventions required to develop expertise at both the individual and the team level' (p. 314).

Alongside training interventions, it is believed that knowledge capture and sharing in the organizations help new professionals to make quick decisions and accelerate their expertise. Baxter (2015) found that proficiency or expertise complex workplace skills like strategic thinking, situational awareness, decision-making, etc. could be accelerated by capturing and using tacit knowledge. Hoffman et al. (2008) support knowledge capture and sharing as a method to accelerate proficiency. However, they also state that 'knowledge management by knowledge capture and knowledge repositories is only a part of the solution to workforce problems' (p. 3-6).

Rosenbaum & Williams (2004) proposed a methodology called *Learning Paths*, to put the structure around haphazard on-the-job activities from day one, eliminate irrelevant activities and sequence on-the-job tasks in a proper order to shorten time to proficiency. A reduction of up to 30% in time to proficiency has been reported (Rosenbaum & Pollock 2015).

## 7.2 MOVING AWAY FROM TRADITIONAL TRAINING TO WORKPLACE LEARNING

In *the TTP study*, the 85 experts were asked to describe 'How the traditional training model looked like before making any changes?' From the analysis, it emerged that most organizations tended to copy models from educational institutions that were more of instructor-centric, content-heavy, classroom training based, but very thin on including job experience. Most of the organizations and institutions depended heavily on contiguous blocks of time to conduct face-to-face, classroom-based or ILT sessions as a primary training mechanism. The goal of such instructor-centric models was to cover the mass of content rather than workplace skills:

> In the old version of the program, we had so much content in there that the real critical things got lost in the content. And it became very difficult for the learner to focus on what is it that's really important really. [project leader]

Major critics of such instructor-centric models were that these models were good enough for delivering a mass of content in a short time but not for developing and accelerating workplace skills. The mass of content actually led to poor retention of skills. The other big challenge of a traditional training model toward accelerating proficiency was a very slow rate of proficiency acquisition and a longer training cycle and a long time to proficiency. Thus, a traditional industrial-era training model fundamentally contradicts the goals of shortening time to proficiency. Several other research studies reported similar limitations of traditional training interventions (e.g., instructor-led or classroom-based training) that lead to longer proficiency acquisition cycle. These limitations included very lengthy training programs required to develop complex skills (Andrews & Fitzgerald 2010); longer training design cycle (Arnold, Ringquist & Prien 1998);

merely textbook problem-solving capabilities (Jonassen & Hung 2008); classroom methodologies disconnected from the workplace realities (Vaughan 2008); need to learn same tasks in the workplace way (Bransford & Schwartz 1999); proficiency requires on-the-job experience (Rosenbaum & Williams 2004). The experts who participated in this study revealed that their organizations were getting away from such traditional classroom-based training models and moving towards workplace learning strategies as a mean to shorten time to proficiency:

> Learning on the workplace became a more conscious choice that resulted in people being more self-sufficient in a shorter period, compared to the previous approach where each skill (general and specific) was packed in the formal (and therefore, a long period of) training. [project leader]

It was noted that training experts increasingly believe that boundaries between learning and workplace need to be diffused. It seems that involvement with the task and emotional loading of tasks amidst the realities of the workplace are the key drivers as to why proficiency gets accelerated in actual workplace settings. One participant summarized it quite realistically as:

> By and large, most things that happen in a training room are fairly ordinary. People are sitting there absorbing stuff, talking about stuff, and it's not an emotional rollercoaster, let's put it that way. Now if they're learning stuff in the workplace, chances are there are a lot more emotions involved. It's more real. It's more immediate. There are other people directly involved. There are consequences for failure or success. All of those things put an emotional loading on whatever is learned and that means that learning will stick more. So in that sense, there's a pretty good chance that it will stick better if it's learned at the point of work rather than in a classroom. But it's not because it's formal or informal, it's because of the way

those memories are encoded and the richness of the
sensory experience that's going on when that encoding
happens. [project leader]

Most of the project leaders appeared to favor on-the-job learning at
the workplace as the biggest contributor to shortening time to
proficiency. The majority of the project leaders mentioned that on-the-
job experience and social interactions at the workplace accounted for
up to 90% of the total learning. This 90% part is mostly instrumental
in increasing the pace of proficiency acquisition. By systematically
leveraging on-the-job workplace learning is fundamental to accelerate
the time to proficiency.

## 7.3  MODEL OF WORKPLACE LEARNING FOR ACCELERATING PROFICIENCY

While there are numerous workplace training and learning strategies
generally deployed in a typical workspace, the research study found
three key training and learning strategies which systematically
leverages various aspects of a workplace to accelerate time to
proficiency of the employees. Most project cases in *the TTP study*
invariably used these three strategies at the workplace to a very high
degree.

The preliminary findings reported in *the TTP study* suggested
leveraging day-to-day workplace activities, job assignments, and tasks,
through three workplace learning to shorten time to proficiency:

1. **MANUFACTURE:** Deliberately manufacturing and structuring
   the experiences not occurring in the usual course of work.
2. **SEQUENCE:** Sequence the activities and experiences in a logical
   but lean learning path by focusing on the most essential activities
   required to achieve the stated proficiency goals.

3. **PERFORMANCE SUPPORT:** Providing necessary just-in-time performance support resources instead of formal training.

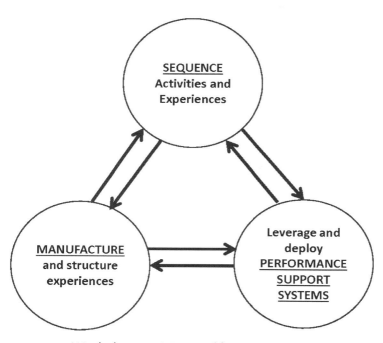

Workplace training and learning space

*Figure 13: Workplace learning framework to shorten time to proficiency (Copyrights Raman K. Attri)*

Figure 13 depicts a circular model of three workplace learning strategies which interact with each other. Though each of these strategies could be successful in isolation, however, time to proficiency is impacted hugely if all three strategies are orchestrated as a system with reasonable mix depending upon the job roles, proficiency goals and support available at the workplace. Three workplace learning and training strategies appear to complement, supplement or strengthen each other at the workplace (as shown by bi-directional interactions with arrows) depending on the job and context.

These three workplace on-the-job learning strategies are described in the following sections.

## 7.4   STRATEGY #1: MANUFACTURE AND STRUCTURE ON-THE-JOB EXPERIENCES

'Professionals learn from real and hard experiences in their jobs. Waiting for experience or an event to occur on its own may lead to a long time to proficiency' [project leader].

Most of the project leaders appeared to have a consensus that professionals learn from real and hard problems they experience in their jobs. However, exposure to various situations is subject to the occurrence of relevant events. If organizations are to wait for events to occur on its own to impart that experience needed to become proficient, it may take a very long time. 'So in effect, if a particular task or a particular event never happens for 12 months, they end up not learning about it' [project leader]. If those experiences are systemically manufactured at the workplace and packed in a compressed time, one could accelerate the time to proficiency by exposing professionals to these experiences at an accelerated rate. For example, one may not encounter a difficult customer very often in sales. However, without having skills to handle such a customer, one may not be deemed proficient. In such a situation, a sales agent could be made to listen to a recorded call of a difficult customer or s/he could be sent along with a senior salesperson in a tough sales call. Thus 'packing experiences in compressed timeframe' is the essence of this strategy: 'Trainees are systematically exposed to situations in a compressed timeframe that it would otherwise take years to experience' [project leader].

A classic example of manufacturing and structuring experiences systematically is by Lesgold et al. (1988; 1991) who reported the success of time the compression strategy with SHERLOCK tutor in which electronics troubleshooting reduced four years of on-the-job training to approximately 25 hours of training. Klein (2003) and DiBello, Missildine & Struttman (2009) also support approach to design experiences in a compressed time. Their method involves recreating an experiential tough-case decision situation at the workplace in the form of 'strategic rehearsals' in which trainees have presented information in a piecemeal fashion about a critical incident as it would unfold in an actual situation, but the entire situation is presented in time-compressed format. This method is considered accelerating expertise in decision-making in a shorter timeframe. Extending it further, Hoffman et al. (2008) presented a strategy called 'tough case time compression' in which a large corpus of rare tough cases is developed and used as training material either in classroom settings or workplace settings (p. 7-3). His premise is that if we can pre-burn the experience in trainees in a compressed timeframe, we may be able to accelerate the time to proficiency.

From the above, we could postulate that rather than waiting for the workplace to provide experiences, if designers can leverage day-to-day routine at the workplace, systematically design experiences and pack those in a compressed timeframe, the time to proficiency could be accelerated.

**Design Guidelines**

- Systematically manufacture the experiences required for a stated proficiency goal.
- Pack the manufactured experiences in a compressed time at the workplace.

- Systematically expose professionals to these experiences at an accelerated rate while doing their jobs.

## 7.5 STRATEGY #2: SEQUENCE THE ACTIVITIES AND EXPERIENCES IN A LEAN LEARNING PATH

'Learning is a process, and just like any other process, we can apply a process improvement approach to eliminate the waste and wasteful time out of the process' [project leader].

An important part of the equation to shorten the time to proficiency appears to be efficient and optimal 'sequencing' of the activities and experiences. The strategy of 'manufacturing the experiences' works better when these experiences are organized, structured, sequenced and packed optimally in a compressed timeframe. 'That time can be shortened by using the taxonomy of cases to establish a learning path that is designed to systematically expose new hires to each of the experiences for which they need to develop proficiency. The experiences can be on-the-job, simulations, or even observations' [project leader]. The activities could be already available in the daily course of business or could be manufactured as indicated by the first strategy. Such an approach to sequencing the activities, tasks, and experiences is called the learning path or pathway. One project leader articulated as 'the basic idea is that when we design learning tasks and then from the analysis of the tasks we think about how to sequence them and simplex to complex from lower to higher or from higher to lower support, so it has to do with structuring the training program in such a way that they best support this process of skill acquisition and knowledge construction' [project leader].

In the context of the complex jobs, Darrah (1996) showed the use of a sequence of organized activities in a computer manufacturing company while Hutchins & Palen (1997) explains it in aviation for the flight engineer's role. The structured on-the-job training (S-OJT) methodology also incorporates a certain level of sequencing and logical flow of work activities for optimal results. There is evidence that such structuring reduces training time (Jacobs & Hawley 2002; Jacobs & Bu-Rahmah 2012; Jacobs 2014). In their book *Learning Paths*, Rosenbaum & Williams (2004, p. 16) advocated an approach to workplace training by 'integrating formal training, practice, and experience along a Learning Path, and not in a topic-by-topic curriculum.' Such an approach entails identifying all existing activities, assignments, tasks, job-aids, on-the-job mentoring opportunities, job-shadowing, and available content, and then sequencing those in the form of learning path based on targeted proficiency definitions. They claim that with such an approach, the organizations can achieve up to 30% reduction in time to proficiency. Thus, a correctly sequenced learning path has a strong potential to reduce time to proficiency. From data analysis, it appears that when activities are carefully sequenced starting from end goal of the program, working backward to the day one of the journey of a learner, it gives a leaner e-learning path that eliminates any activities not required for the end goal. The underlying philosophy is to design a path to include only the most essential learning outcomes and then map the most essential activities to achieve those outcomes. 'This accelerated experiential learning process is very much, what's the learning outcome? Now, what activities do I need to send them to do in order to get the learning?' [project leader].

This study supports the technique to assign the time target to each activity on the learning path, as mentioned by Rosenbaum & Williams (2004). By doing so, the total time to proficiency can be estimated and tracked and then focused efforts can be made to shorten the time. 'You're going to have [to] master three things and you [are] working on these others and so it becomes part of an ongoing assessment' [project leader].

While still taking the 'time' out of the sequence, this technique allows designers to be conscious of the spacing and interval required for practice, as well as reflection and feedback to ensure the sustained transfer of learning. Such spaced practice and intervals are considered very important ingredients for long-term learning transfer to the workplace (Birnbaum et al. 2013; Davachi et al. 2010; Karpicke & Bauernschmidt 2011; Thalheimer 2006).

As suggested in Chapter 5, the sequencing is made more efficient by ensuring that learns start from learning events or activities that happen more frequently, start with low complexity tasks and progress towards higher complexity and start from simpler tasks towards more difficult tasks. Such criteria make sequencing more optimal. In regards to criteria for sequencing, Arnold & Collier (2013) demonstrated that complex decision-making skills of novice-level professional knowledge workers were accelerated when they are presented with the 'authentic cases' which 'gradually increases in complexity systematically extending procedural knowledge from case to case' (p. 7).

Thus, time to proficiency could be accelerated by sequencing of available (or manufactured) activities in a learning path according to certain criteria, assigning time targets to activities and then packing the sequence in a compressed timeframe.

## Design Guidelines

- Identify all possible activities, opportunities in natural settings.
- Select the most essential activities required to achieve stated proficiency.
- Sequence the experiences to achieve the stated proficiency goal in the shortest possible time.
- Use criteria based sequencing.
- Assign milestones and dates.

- Design a "lean" learning path by eliminating redundant, irrelevant or wasteful activities.

## 7.6 STRATEGY #3. DEPLOY PERFORMANCE SUPPORT SYSTEMS AND RESOURCES

'Proficiency is accelerated when learning happens closer to or at the point of need' [project leader].

The third strategy that is revealed by study advocates increasing the use of PSS. PSS are mostly electronics resources like online learning content, reference material, knowledge-base, procedures, mobile applications, decision-making software, etc. which can provide just-in-time training or just-in-time support. 'Performance support simply means at the moment of need you have it available' [project leader]. This research showed that organizations are deploying more PSS in place of or in augmentation of training to induct a culture where learning is self-driven 'as employees seek assistance on-the-job from the EPSS' [project leader]. With the availability of new technologies, shape and extent of PSS are also changing beyond its original role of just-in-time resource for training or support or information. For example, Andrews (2004), based on a framework by Rosenberg (2001), proposes that 'the related constructs of "training," "knowledge management" and "performance support" can interact to form a strong HPT [Human Performance Technology] toolset. All three constructs are crucial in building a learning organization' (p. 7). Such a performance support system provides crucial support during a rare event that either lacks systematic training or when learners have forgotten how to do a low-frequency task. Nguyen (2006) points out that as one progresses from novice to expert, as training interventions go down, there should be an increase in the use of EPSS.

A PSS deployed to deliver learning or information at the moment of need actually accelerates time to proficiency because employees can access the resources at their own pace, rather than at the pace of the instructor or the pace of information flow from their colleagues. It is also noticed that PSS can be used as a reference resource or delivery media inside the formal training class. As stated in Chapter 5, PSS could supplement or even replace any formal training intervention if it is deployed correctly. Such strategic use of EPSS allows instructor-led training to focus on those skills which can be impacted only in face-to-face settings. Gery (1991) suggested using EPSS for individualized online access to reduce content-heavy training. The newer PSS also get integrated with other systems and can either send the reminders or can send the refresh boosters to the learners. While the literature does not directly specify if and how EPSS accelerate proficiency, one key inference drawn from *the TTP study* is that when proficiency goals are viewed holistically, then training, non-training and performance support solutions may be able to complement each other to accelerate the time to proficiency.

**Design Guidelines**

- Identify the suite of resources which act as PSS (electronics or non-electronics resources, networking, job-aids, software help, e-learning courses, etc.).
- Make resources available online or otherwise at the point of need as just-in-time training or just-in-time support.
- Self-paced access to resources supports, augments or replaces content-driven formal training.
- Spaced reinforcement of learning through automated means.

## 7.7 SUMMARY OF RECOMMENDATIONS

While designing workplace learning interventions, the learning and training designers could use some of the following guidelines to accelerate time to proficiency of employees by implementing three strategies discussed in this chapter:

- Define the proficiency indicators or measures for the job role. Analyze the existing formal classroom-based training or other training interventions currently being used in the organization. Based on the endpoint proficiency goals, map all the available activities, tasks and assignments done day-to-day routine and assess how each stated proficiency goal can be achieved through those activities.

- Assess already available PSS, job-aids, online knowledge-base repositories, and other electronic resources to assess if any of the training requirements can be eliminated and if resources can be used instead to achieve the same proficiency goal.

- Rethink redeployment of existing PSS or design new PSS to deliver some content, information or training instead of long formal training programs. The analysis may involve the availability of any e-learning or other training courses if certain outcomes are achieved best through those opportunities.

- 'Manufacture' or design any other experience or activity necessary to reach the target proficiency, but not occurring frequently enough at the workplace in the usual course of work.

- Sequence the activities in a logical order to achieve targeted time to proficiency goals in the shortest time. Have different criteria like frequency, complexity, difficulty, and usage of the skill to create an optimal and logical sequence of activities. During sequencing, any irrelevant activities not leading to stated proficiency goals is eliminated.

- Assign milestone or time target for each activity based on overall time to proficiency goals for a given job.

# CHAPTER 8

# A TRAINING DESIGN MODEL FOR ACCELERATED PROFICIENCY

Previous chapters outlined significant patterns that were observed in *the TTP study*. Chapter 4 explained five e-learning strategies to design an e-learning curriculum which holds the potential to accelerate proficiency in terms of initial readiness. Chapter 5 focused on five instructional strategies which leveraged both e-learning and workplace challenges to deliver a classroom or formal training to accelerate the acquisition of highly complex skills. Chapter 6 described a model and three workplace learning design strategies for the events or skills that must leverage the job assignments. These preliminary findings have shown the encouraging potential training holds to accelerate the proficiency of employees. However, the findings were described in the silos of e-learning, classroom, and on-the-job learning. This chapter intends to combine findings into a full picture, in an attempt to suggest a simplified instructional model based on four phases of proficiency growth.

## 8.1 SUMMARY OF STRATEGIES: ONLINE, CLASSROOM AND WORKPLACE LEARNING

In the previous chapters, the following 13 strategies were outlined. Each strategy may have its own effect and contribution toward an effective training design that may shorten time to readiness of the learners.

**E-learning/Online Strategies**

- Strategy #1: Experience-rich and multi-technology mix
- Strategy #2: Time-spaced microlearning content
- Strategy #3: Scenario-based contextualization of e-learning
- Strategy #4: On-demand electronic performance support systems
- Strategy #5: Optimally sequenced e-learning path

**Classroom/Instructional Strategies**

- Strategy #1: Segmentation of critical tasks
- Strategy #2: Self-guided pre-work/preparation
- Strategy #3: Contextualize learning with scenarios
- Strategy #4: Emotional loading/emotional involvement
- Strategy #5: Spaced distributed chunked interventions

**Workplace/On-the-job Learning Strategies**

- Strategy #1: Manufacture and structure on-the-job experiences
- Strategy #2: Sequence the activities and experiences in a lean learning path
- Strategy #3. Deploy performance support systems and resources

## 8.2 A FULL PICTURE OF TRAINING DESIGN FOR ACCELERATED PROFICIENCY

While all of these strategies were presented in their silos based on the nature of learning, there is quite an overlap among strategies in terms of their intent and underlying philosophy. Some of those commonalities are listed here:

Segmentation of tasks appeared as a strategy in the context of classroom instruction. However, its essence goes back to the basic instructional design. The strategy advocates using data to segment the nature of the tasks base don their characteristics. The idea is to determine, what needs to be learned first, what can be learned in self-paced mode and what must be learned on the job, what can be provided through PSS and what must require formal training. Thus before any design is put in place, it is absolutely necessary to understand the nature of tasks/skills involved to do a given job. Thus, this is a strategy that fundamentally determines e-learning, classroom, and on-the-job learning design.

Correctly segmented tasks/skills allow to optimally sequence the activities through which those tasks/skills are learned, leading to the development of an efficient learning path. This strategy holds the most potential in cutting out the significant time from the learning journey of the learners. This strategy has an application for both optimizing the e-learning as well as on-the-job learning.

The sequenced learning sessions are more effective when those are chunked into smaller sessions or converted into microlearning sessions, which are then time-spaced and distributed. This strategy is essential in both e-learning design as well as classroom training design.

Contextualization of learning through scenarios is a powerful strategy for designing e-learning as well as classroom instructional design for complex skill learning. This strategy allows learners actively involve during online as well as in the formal training in the process of solving realistic problems they may encounter at the job. Such preemptive involvement again contributes towards preparing learners who become proficient faster when deployed on the job.

Deliberately manufacturing and structuring on-the-job experiences/ activities is a strategy that is geared toward workplace learning design only. However, it leverages foundational concept such as segmenting the tasks which are appropriate for on-the-job learning, contextualizing the learning through realistic assignment at work, time-spacing or distributing those identified activities and develop an efficient learning sequence out of that to structure experience that contributes directly toward reducing time to proficiency.

No matter the phase of learning, preILT, ILT or post-ILT, actively involving the learners into the learning which exert emotional loading onto the learners and trigger emotional involvement, goes a long way toward accelerating time to proficiency.

Last but not the least, deploying on-demand performance support systems is a promising e-learning strategy as well as an important workplace learning strategy that showed the most significant potential to replace or reduce the amount of formal training. Though in usual instructional design, performance support typically is viewed as a resource, in the new model it is viewed as the foremost strategy that can determine what to train upon and what to provide support upon.

The other strategies like self-guided pre-work and multi-channel delivery modes for experience-rich are two strategies which are e-learning in nature. If used properly, these strategies may have some noticeable impact on designing training which is effective in shortening time to proficiency.

It must be noted that no single training and learning strategy might be powerful enough to impact the overall time to proficiency of the learners. However, when these strategies work in tandem with each other, the overall impact might be amplified. While training might be a smaller portion of overall efforts to reduce time to proficiency, a bad training design may basically hamper acceleration. This was discussed in chapter 4 that showed how inefficient training design may lead to a longer time to proficiency instead. Thus it is important to orchestrate these training design strategies in such a way that training acts an enabler toward accelerating proficiency.

In a nutshell, combining all the above strategies lead to the following nine strategies when training design is viewed holistically:

    **(1)  Segmentation of critical tasks**
    **(2)  Optimally sequenced learning path**
    **(3)  Self-guided pre-work**
    **(4)  Contextualized learning with scenarios**
    **(5)  Emotional loading and involvement**
    **(6)  Multi-channel experience-rich delivery modes**
    **(7)  Manufactured and structured on-the-job experiences**
    **(8)  Time-spaced distributed microlearning**
    **(9)  On-demand performance support systems**

These nine training and learning strategies are shown in figure 14 in the form of four phases of proficiency growth that was discussed in Chapter 3.

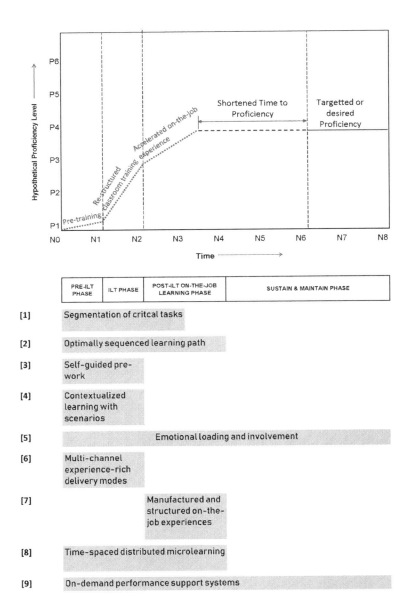

*Figure 14: Training design model for accelerated proficiency with nine strategies (image copyrights Raman K. Attri)*

While segmentation of tasks should be done before any training is delivered, the segmentation determines what goes in at different phases like pre-ILT, ILT and post-ILT phase. The well-sequenced learning path determines the activities and their order a learner would undergo from day one of learner's proficiency acquisition journey, until he reaches the desired proficiency. Thus, this strategy is all prevailing throughout proficiency growth.

The self-guided pre-work finds its central utilization in the pre-ILT phase whereby it holds the potential to uplift the proficiency level of learners before they are introduced to classroom-based formal training interventions. Also, the formal training sessions should leverage self-guided homework that allows learners to ingress a deeper level of learning.

No matter it is e-learning or classroom training, both must be designed with strong contextualization using scenarios from real job challenges and pressing problems one may encounter on the job. Using this strategy for training design in the pre-ILT and ILT phase is very important. This strategy also ensures necessary emotional loading and involvement which is triggered when pressure and consequences are built into the learning. The emotional loading is an effective strategy that may have one of the most significant impacts throughout the proficiency acquisition journey in terms of how fast learners come up to speed. The emotional loading needs to be designed into all the interventions throughout the proficiency acquisition journey while the job itself will introduce constant emotional loading when a learner has acquired desired proficiency in a given job role.

Leveraging on-the-job assignments is an extremely critical training design strategy which typically gets a back seat in traditional instructional design. The level of emotional loading experienced by the learners also depends on how sound the on-the-job experiences are designed, manufactured and structured. In fact, the key to shortening time to proficiency lies in how well the job is leveraged as a training delivery channel.

At the end of the day, learners need to be provided with learning and experiences through experience-rich and multi-channel modes that allow efficient transfer of information. Such a strategy leverages the latest and greatest technologies. Technologies also ensure time-spaced, distributed learning in smaller chunks. The newer technologies allow using microlearning, on-demand performance support systems and learning management systems to integrate these strategies seamlessly.

Above all, on-demand performance support systems must be deployed throughout the proficiency acquisition journey and after that as well. The performance support systems should become the primary mechanism of learning to maintain proficiency on the tasks which one may not encounter all the time.

Figure 14 depicts the juxtaposition of strategies over four phases of proficiency acquisition. The model is built based on the combined holistic trajectory of proficiency acquisition (discussed inc chapter 3) which specifies to lift the proficiency curve slightly during the pre-ILT phase and then lift the exit proficiency level during ILT phase, while learner acquires proficiency at a higher rate during the post-ILT on-the-job learning phase.

## 8.3    PROFICIENCY FOR A JOB ROLE, NOT TASKS

While the attainment of proficiency acquisition has been treated as a single event that happens at a specific time, it must be noted that an individual is expected to learn a range of skills, knowledge, behaviors, tasks in order to perform a given job role. During the proficiency acquisition journey, a learner's proficiency in different tasks may vary, but his ability to do the job as a whole will still have specific progress. Proficiency, ultimately, is the ability to produce the job-specific deliverables, which in turn may require different combinations of skills at different proficiency level. In this book, proficiency is viewed on a job role level and not at a given task level. To perform a job proficiently, one does not have to learn all the skills upfront or at least are not required to be mastered equally (Attri 2018).

# CHAPTER 9

# ACCELERATING PROFICIENCY IS BEYOND DESIGNING TRAINING

Previous chapters outlined major findings in *the TTP study* in relationship to training and learning design. Chapter 8 combined the strategies discussed in Chapter 4 on online e-learning design, Chapter 5 on classroom instructional strategies and Chapter 6 on workplace learning design strategies. These preliminary findings and the associated preliminary models have shown good potential to accelerate the proficiency of employees. Chapter 8 presented a holistic model which argues that if all the nine strategies are orchestrated as a system, it may lead to an effective training design that puts learners on an accelerated path towards the desired proficiency in their job roles. However, the contribution of training design cannot be emphasized in isolation. This chapter intends to conclude the final observations from the overarching model of speed to proficiency and put the role of training toward shortening time to proficiency in perspective.

## 9.1 PUTTING TRAINING IN PERSPECTIVE: SKILL ACQUISITION VERSUS ATTAINING PROFICIENCY

Over 85 project leaders who were interviewed emphasized that proficiency is a state or level of performance of achieving business outcomes to pre-established standards consistently. They differentiated it from being good in some skills, knowledge or attitude or ability to perform some activities, steps or tasks. The findings suggest that proficiency is about results rather than about demonstrating a skill, task or activity. Certainly, without knowledge, skills, and behaviors and without the ability to perform required tasks, procedures or activities, it is not feasible to produce the desired outcomes. Fred (2002, p. 43) perhaps suggested the closest relationship of knowledge and the outcome, and valued the outcomes that come out of learning knowledge: 'The proficiency threshold, therefore, is the exact moment when a worker can convert knowledge through action into the promised value for the customer.' However, being able to produce the designated results independently ultimately determines whether or not someone is proficient, and if not there yet, how soon s/he could be in that state.

Attaining the consistent performance within the complexity of the workplace require not only skills, knowledge, and behaviors, but also requires several other support mechanisms and interventions. 'You really need to be clear about what's the business point, not what people need to learn, but what needs to happen for the business, or how do they need to perform' [project leader]. The focus should be on enabling learners on how to produce the business outcomes that mattered most to the organizations. This observation supports the viewpoint of performance paradigm in human resource development (HRD) in terms of enhancing total individual performance, not just by training interventions but also by other interventions (Clark 2008; Swanson & Holton III 2001).

Among key findings, some project leaders mentioned that the dynamics inside the training process were not representative of what happens in the real world in terms of pressure, consequences, goals, and experience. Project leaders stoutly iterated that performance during a training event was a false indicator of an individual's proficiency. They also recognized that not all of the performance seen in any training event would transfer to the job towards accelerating proficiency. 'Performance during the acquisition process is misleading, and in many situations, that's the only thing that people [responsible for training] are going to see - the performance during training' [project leader]. Soderstrom & Bjork (2015), Chevalier (2004)and Stolovitch (2000) argued that performance during training interventions could be a misleading indicator of proficiency and long-term learning of behaviors that should persist in the workplace. 'When you think about really learning to do something to a level of performance or a level of proficiency, it takes a lot more than that and that's what people kind of fall short [of] as they say' [study particicpant]. Unless the performers are prepared to produce business outcomes in a shorter time, training may not contribute toward accelerating proficiency.

## 9.2 SOLUTIONS TO ACCELERATED PROFICIENCY ARE BEYOND MERELY TRAINING

While modern studies emphasize aligning training objectives with business needs and goals (Hughes 2003; Saks, Haccoun & Belcourt 2010; Salas et al. 2012), preparing performers toward proficiency in a shorter time appears to be beyond the reach of any instructional design models, just because instructional design models tend to focus on knowledge, skills, and behaviors. Managers typically consider training as the only solution to all performance and proficiency problems. In *the TTP study,* almost all the project leaders unanimously advocated that while training helps with initial readiness and understanding the job, training is not a solution for developing or accelerating proficiency. 'The training has only one value, and that is to improve skills and knowledge. That's all it does' [project leader]. The project leaders went on emphasizing how small a part training plays in the overall equation of performance improvement: 'Training is usually one of the more insignificant ones' [project leader]. Accelerating proficiency requires not only training-related solutions but also non-training solutions.

Baker (2017) argued that in modern organizations the assumption that a technically superior workforce is the key to organizational performance tended to gear all solutions to being skill-focused or training-focused. Some researchers also argue that in general, training is just an event with a specific purpose to deliver the necessary skills or behaviors, and usually, it has a specific assessment checkpoint that signals its end. Producing results or waiting till results are produced is usually not the goal of training interventions and is indeed not feasible. Leading practitioners Pollock, Wick & Jefferson (2015, p. 41) asserted that performance is the result of the interaction of the worker, work, and workplace, but the '[t]raining impacts worker only.' Training is useful only if it focuses on developing performers to produce business results. 'In this model [of accelerated proficiency], training is complete only when the learner has achieved proficiency... it was much more focused on how to help this learner become proficient in their job as quickly as possible so that they are contributing to the overall roles of the organization' [project leader].

The findings in this study showed that the strategies to accelerated proficiency extend much beyond training or learning interventions. 'The real answer to compressing time-to-competence is that one has to look outside of the training – look at what's wrapped around it' [project leader]. Almost all the project leaders advocated that training alone was not the solution to accelerate proficiency. Project leaders viewed training as one of many solutions, and they used a range of non-training solutions as well, which altogether appeared to reduce time to proficiency. 'Training isn't the answer in every situation, and for many situations, you need a very different strategy as the main approach to getting people to the point when they are competent' [project leader]. The findings of *the TTP study* positions training as one of the several possible solutions to accelerate proficiency, rather than the total solution in itself. 'Training very rarely will result in desired performance; that it takes a number of different interventions, all woven together to produce an outcome' [project leader]. This closely aligns with the practices of human performance technology (Kang 2017; Marker et al. 2014; Pershing 2006; Van Tiem, Moseley & Dessinger 2012; Wallace 2006). This is aligned with the observations made by Swanson & Holton III (2001) and Dean (2016) with regard to the need to use several non-linear interventions in addition to learning interventions to attain desired performance.

Further, project leaders clarified that accelerated proficiency is nor about speeding up the learning curve of a specific individual, neither is it just learning or training a given content in a shorter time. The goal of accelerated proficiency was seen as reducing the total time taken to reach the state of proficiency, rather than reducing the training duration alone. In the majority of the project cases, achieving the state of proficiency took several times more time than the duration of the training interventions used. 'Do[ing] the week's program in a day – *[sic]* and that's not we're talking about. We're talking about the 18 months' target [and] moving that down to 12 months' [project leader]. Thus, the goals of accelerated proficiency are not described in terms of learning knowledge or skill.

## 9.3 CRITICAL ROLE OF TRAINING IS UNDENIABLE

However, the value of training in skill acquisition and knowledge acquisition was not undermined by any project leader. Some of them even believed that the primary goal of a training intervention should be to reduce time to proficiency. 'If training isn't shortening the time, then maybe they shouldn't be doing it. It should always shorten the time' [project leader]. Admittedly, training is a critical part of most performance improvement interventions (Clark 2008; Kraiger 2014). There are cases in which desired proficiency can be attained in training settings, or training is the only viable, practical option; for example, job roles in which life and safety matter (military, pilots, surgeons, firefighters, etc.) and failure is no option in real situations (Hintze 2008; Jenkins et al. 2016; Klein & Borders 2016; Kuchenbrod 2016). Alternatively, training may be more feasible solutions in the job roles that are not readily measured in terms of immediate on-the-job outcomes (e.g., roles related to business strategy), or job roles are governed by some licensing or other regulatory norms (e.g., oil and gas related jobs). Such situations may necessitate training as a fail-safe mechanism or even a mandatory requirement (Crichton & Flin 2004). In *the TTP study*, it was seen that in the instances where training was designed, the focus was on making performers produce the desired business outcomes that mattered most to the organization (as opposed to improving or accelerating their task performance by imparting certain skills to them). Training did not seem to end until that state was achieved. In that perspective that training was considered as a small part of the overall solution, the traditional instructional design processes appeared to have rendered outcomes that were not required or not immediately useful; and in some cases, they even caused a bottleneck that slowed down the rate of proficiency.

There is no doubt that learning is an underlying process in all the endeavors undertaken by an individual in the workplace (Saks, Haccoun & Belcourt 2010; Salas et al. 2012). Nevertheless, what is being measured and how success is reported are matters of perspective.

While training and learning are the core mechanisms of professional development, skill acquisition and expertise development in organizations, a goal to strategically leverage training and learning efforts to shorten time to proficiency remains the prime concern of business leaders. Hoffman et al. (2014) have put together the most recent synthesis of over last three decades of research in their book *Accelerated Expertise: Training for High Proficiency in a Complex World* as an authentic source of training methods from research that have demonstrated evidence of accelerating high proficiency. The findings, strategies, and methods discussed in the author's this book provide affirmations and support to several of the methods Hoffman et al. (2014) discussed or proposed.

The findings and recommendations suggested in previous chapters may find important applications in designing classroom training, e-learning courseware and workplace learning interventions in such a way that either accelerates or at least optimizes time to proficiency of the workforce.

## 9.4    MODEL OF SPEED TO PROFICIENCY: TOTAL PROFICIENCY ECO-SYSTEM

While the focus of this book was to present training and learning strategies which were found promising in accelerating time to proficiency at the workplace, *the TTP study* concluded that training alone rarely leads to accelerating proficiency; it requires solutions beyond training. One of the most important takeaways from *the TTP study* was that proficiency can be accelerated only when the right conditions in the form of a total eco-system is ensured.

The final analysis showed that the majority of project cases used six business-level practices with a high degree of prevalence to shorten time to proficiency of employees in various contexts. These six business practices, as shown in figure 15, were:

(1) Defining business-driven proficiency measures in terms of expected business outcomes from a job role;

(2) Developing a proficiency reference map of all the inputs, conditions and roadblocks that determine or influence how required business outcomes are being produced in a job role;

(3) Sequencing an efficient proficiency path of activities and experiences ordered to produce the desired business outcomes in the shortest possible time;

(4) Manufacturing accelerated contextual experiences by leveraging on-the-job opportunities or training interventions in a compressed timeframe;

(5) Promoting an active emotional immersion through engagements, consequences, stakes, feedback and proficiency assessments; and

(6) Setting up a proficiency eco-system, providing timely support to performers while doing the job such as enabling job environment, highly involved manager, structured mentoring from experts, purposeful social connectivity with peers, leveraging subject matter experts and on-demand performance support systems.

*Figure 15: Six business practices to shorten time to proficiency in S2Pro© Model of Accelerated Proficiency (image copyrights Raman K. Attri)*

Organizations orchestrated these six business practices as an input-output-feedback system to reduce time to proficiency of the workforce. A conceptual model (*Accelerated Proficiency Model* or S2Pro© *model of speed to proficiency*) was developed representing interactions among six business-level practices/processes as a closed-loop system to explain the concept and process of accelerated proficiency in the workplace.

It was seen that across the board, these practices were implemented through twenty-four strategies proven successful in various workplace contexts. The strategies employed were much beyond the boundaries of conventional training interventions, while the job itself acted as the primary mechanism to accelerate proficiency. A two-level hierarchical framework (*6/24 framework of strategies*) was also constructed in the form of a checklist consisting of six practices and twenty-four strategies for practitioners.

Overall findings and final model of accelerated proficiency are published in other publications title "*Model Of Accelerated Proficiency In The Workplace: Six Core Concepts To Shorten Time-To-Proficiency of Employees*"[9] (Attri & Wu 2017; 2018). The above mentioned six business practices, twenty-four strategies and the model of speed to proficiency are described in details in the forthcoming publications[10].

[9] Published as Attri, RK & Wu, WS 2018, "Model of accelerated proficiency in the workplace: six core concepts to shorten time-to-proficiency of employees," *Asia Pacific Journal of Advanced Business and Social Studies*, vol. 4, no. 1, http://dx.doi.org/10.25275/apjabssv4i1bus1.

[10] Interested reader may check out author's doctorate theiss (no public access until July 2019). Attri, RK 2018, "Modelling accelerated proficiency in organisations: practices and strategies to shorten," PhD thesis, Southern Cross University, Lismore, Australia.

# RELEVANT PUBLICATIONS BY THE AUTHOR

1. Attri, RK 2018, *Accelerate your leadership development in training domain: Proven success strategies for new training & learning managers*, Speed To Proficiency Research: S2Pro©, Singapore, available at <https://www.amazon.com/ /dp/9811400660/>.

2. Attri, RK 2014, "Rethinking professional skill development in competitive corporate world: accelerating time-to-expertise of employees at workplace," in J Latzo (ed.), *Proceedings of Conference on Education and Human Development in Asia*, Hiroshima, 2-4 March, PRESDA Foundation, Kitanagova, pp. 1–11, http://dx.doi.org/10.13140/RG.2.1.5125.7043.

3. Attri, RK 2018, "Modelling accelerated proficiency in organisations: practices and strategies to shorten," PhD thesis, Southern Cross University, Lismore, Australia.

4. Attri, RK & Wu, WS 2018, "Model of accelerated proficiency in the workplace: six core concepts to shorten time-to-proficiency of employees," *Asia Pacific Journal of Advanced Business and Social Studies*, vol. 4, no. 1, http://dx.doi.org/10.25275/apjabssv4i1bus1.

5. Attri, RK & Wu, WS 2017, "Model of accelerated proficiency in the workplace: six core concepts to shorten time-to-proficiency of employees," *First Australia and New Zealand Conference on Advanced Research (ANZCAR)*, Melbourne, Asia Pacific Institute of Advanced Research, Melbourne, 17-18 June, pp. 1-10, viewed 24 July 2017, <http://apiar.org.au/wp-content/uploads/2017/07/1_ANZCAR_2017_BRR713_Bus-1-10.pdf>.

6. Attri, R. K. & Wu, W. S. (2015). E-Learning Strategies to Accelerate Time-to-Proficiency in Acquiring Complex Skills: Preliminary Findings. Paper presented at *E-learning Forum Asia Conference*, Jun 2015. Singapore: SIM University, available at <https://www.researchgate.net/publication/282647943>.

7. Attri, RK & Wu, W 2015, 'Conceptual model of workplace training and learning strategies to shorten time-to-proficiency in complex skills: preliminary findings', paper presented to the *9th International Conference on Researching in Work and Learning (RWL)*, Singapore, 9-11 December, viewed 24 June 2017, <https://www.researchgate.net/publication/286623558>.

8. Attri, RK & Wu, WS 2016a, "Classroom-based instructional strategies to accelerate proficiency of employees in complex job skills," paper presented to the Asian American Conference for Education, Singapore, 15-16 January, viewed 24 June 2017, <https://www.researchgate.net/publication/303803099>.

9. Attri, RK & Wu, WS 2016b, "E-learning strategies at workplace that support speed to proficiency in complex skills," in M Rozhan and N Zainuddin (eds.), *Proceedings of the 11th International Conference on E-Learning: ICEl2016*, Kuala Lampur, 2-3 June, Academic Conference and Publishing, Reading, pp. 176–184, viewed 24 June 2017, <https://www.researchgate.net/publication/303802961>.

# REFERENCES

Accenture 2013, *Top-Five Focus Areas for Improving Sales Effectiveness Initiatives*, viewed 24 June 2017, <https://www.accenture.com/t20150523T052741__w__/us-en/_acnmedia/Accenture/Conversion-Assets/DotCom/Documents/Global/PDF/Strategy_4/Accenture-Top-Five-Improvements-Sales-Effectiveness.pdf>.

Alorica 2017, "Think quick: increase speed to proficiency," viewed 24 June 2018, <https://www.alorica.com/wp-content/uploads/2017/09/ebook_SpeedtoProficiency.pdf>.

Andrews, DH 2004, "Advanced training technologies and their impact on human performance improvement," *The RTO Human Factors and Medicine Panel (HFM) Symposium: Advanced Technologies for Military Training*, Genoa, Italy, Research and Technology Organization (RTO) of North Atlantic Treaty Organization (NATO), Cedex, France, pp. 1–11, http://dx.doi.org/10.14339/RTO-MP-HFM-101.

Andrews, DH & Fitzgerald, P 2010, "Accelerating learning of competence and increasing long-term learning retention," paper presented to the ITEC Conference, London, viewed 24 June 2017, <http://www.dtic.mil/cgi-bin/GetTRDoc?AD=ADA522088>.

Angelo, RL, Ryu, RK, Pedowitz, RA, Beach, W, Burns, J, Dodds, J, Field, L, Getelman, M, Hobgood, R, McIntyre, L & others 2015, "A proficiency-based progression training curriculum coupled with a model simulator results in the acquisition of a superior arthroscopic bankart skill set," *Arthroscopy: The Journal of Arthroscopic & Related Surgery*, vol. 31, no. 10, pp. 1854–1871, viewed 24 June 2017, <https://www.ucc.ie/en/media/academic/assertforhealth/assertdocs/1.1-s2.0-S0749806315005836-main.pdf>.

Arnold, DE, Ringquist, JJ & Prien, K 1998, "Reducing the cycle time of training and development in organizations," *Journal of Cycle Time Research*, pp. 21–30, viewed 24 June 2017, <http://citeseerx.ist.psu.edu/viewdoc/download?doi=10.1.1.508.9235&rep=rep1&type=pdf>.

Arnold, V & Collier, P 2013, "Incase: simulating experience to accelerate expertise development by knowledge workers," *Intelligent Systems in Accounting and Financial Management*, vol. 20, no. 1, pp. 1–21, http://dx.doi.org/10.1002/isaf.

ASTD 2014, *2014 State of the Industry*, ASTD, viewed 24 June 2017, <https://www.td.org/Publications/Research-Reports/2014/2014-State-of-the-Industry?mktcops=c.learning-and-development\textasciitidlec.lt\textasciitidlec.sr-leader\textasciitidlec.learning-and-development>.

Attri, RK 2014, "Rethinking professional skill development in competitive corporate world: accelerating time-to-expertise of employees at workplace," in J Latzo (ed.), *Proceedings of Conference on Education and Human Development in Asia*, Hiroshima, 2-4 March, PRESDA Foundation, Kitanagova, pp. 1–11, http://dx.doi.org/10.13140/RG.2.1.5125.7043.

_____ 2018, "Modelling accelerated proficiency in organisations: practices and strategies to shorten," PhD thesis, Southern Cross University, Lismore, Australia.

Attri, RK & Wu, W 2015, "Conceptual model of workplace training and learning strategies to shorten time-to-proficiency in complex skills: preliminary findings," *9th International Conference on Researching in Work and Learning (RWL) Conference*, Singapore, Institute for Adult Learning, Singapore, viewed 24 June 2017, <http://www.rwl2015.com/papers/Paper100.pdf>.

_____ 2016a, "Classroom-based instructional strategies to accelerate proficiency of employees in complex job skills," paper presented to the Asian American Conference for Education, Singapore, viewed 24 June 2017, <https://www.researchgate.net/publication/303803099>.

_____ 2016b, "E-learning strategies at workplace that support speed to proficiency in complex skills," in M Rozhan and N Zainuddin (ed.), *Proceedings of the 11th International Conference on E-Learning: ICEl2016*, Kuala Lampur, 2-3 June, Academic Conference and Publishing, Reading, pp. 176–184, viewed 24 June 2017, <https://www.researchgate.net/publication/303802961>.

Bachlechner, D, Kohlegger, M, Maier, R & Waldhart, G 2010, "Taking pressure off knowledge workers with the help of situational applications-improving time-to-proficiency in knowledge work settings," in A Fred & J Filipe (ed.), *Proceedings of the International Conference on Knowledge Management and Information Sharing (KMIS-2010)*, Valencia, 25-28 October, SCITEPRESS Science and Technology, Setúbal, Portugal, pp. 378–381, http://dx.doi.org/10.5220/0003118203780381.

Backus, C, Keegan, K, Gluck, C & Gulick, LMV 2010, "Accelerating leadership development via immersive learning and cognitive apprenticeship," *International Journal of Training and Development*, vol. 14, no. 2, pp. 144–148, http://dx.doi.org/10.1111/j.1468-2419.2010.00347.x.

Baker, T 2017, Management myth# 7—a technically superior workforce is a pathway to a high-performing business, in *Performance Management for Agile Organizations*, Springer, Cham, pp. 159–173, http://dx.doi.org/10.1007/978-3-319-40153-9_10.

Barbian, J 2002, "A little help from your friends," *Training*, vol. 39, no. 3, p. 38.

Baxter, HC 2015, "Specialized knowledge transfer: accelerating the expertise development cycle," *Procedia Manufacturing*, vol. 3, pp. 1465–1472, http://dx.doi.org/10.1016/j.promfg.2015.07.323.

Billett, S 1996, "Towards a model of workplace learning: the learning curriculum," *Studies in Continuing Education*, vol. 18, no. 1, pp. 43–58, http://dx.doi.org/10.1080/0158037960180103.

Birnbaum, MS, Kornell, N, Bjork, EL & Bjork, R A 2013, "Why interleaving enhances inductive learning: the roles of discrimination and retrieval," *Memory & Cognition*, vol. 41, no. 3, pp. 392–402, http://dx.doi.org/10.3758/s13421-012-0272-7.

Bjork, EL & Bjork, RA 2011, Making things hard on yourself, but in a good way: creating desirable difficulties to enhance learning, in M Gernsbacher, R Pew, L Hough & J Pomerantz (ed.), *Psychology and the real world: Essays illustrating fundamental contributions to society*, Worth, New York, pp. 55–64, viewed 24 June 2017, <https://bjorklab.psych.ucla.edu/wp-content/uploads/sites/13/2016/04/EBjork_RBjork_2011.pdf>.

Bjork, RA 2013, Desirable difficulties perspective on learning, in H Pashler (ed.), *Encyclopedia of the mind*, SAGE, Thousand Oaks, pp. 243–245, http://dx.doi.org/10.4135/9781452257044.n88.

Bjork, RA & Linn, M 2006, "The science of learning and the learning of science: introducing desirable difficulties," *APS Observer*, vol. 19, no. 3, pp. 6–7, viewed 24 June 2017, <https://www.researchgate.net/profile/Robert_Bjork/publication/237420547>.

Bloom, BS 1968, "Learning for mastery," *UCLA Evaluation Comment*, vol. 1, no. 2, pp. 1–12, viewed 24 June 2017, <http://ruby.fgcu.edu/courses/ikohn/summer/pdffiles/learnmastery2.pdf>.

Bologa, R & Lupu, AR 2007, "Accelerating the sharing of knowledge in order to speed up the process of enlarging software development teams - a practical example," in C Long, V Mladenov & Z Bojkovic (ed.), *Proceedings of the 6th WSEAS International Conference on Artificial Intelligence, Knowledge Engineering and Data Bases*, Corfu Island, Greece, World Scientific and Engineering Academy and Society, pp. 90–95, viewed 24 June 2017, <http://www.wseas.us/e-library/conferences/2007corfu/papers/540-225.pdf>.

Borton, G 2007, "Managing productivity: measuring the business impact of employee proficiency and the employee job life cycle," *Management Services*, no. 7, pp. 28–33, viewed 24 June 2017, <http://www.ims-productivity.com/user/custom/journal/2007/autumn/IMSaut07pg28-33.pdf>.

Bower, M, Dalgarno, B, Kennedy, GE, Lee, MJ & Kenney, J 2015, "Design and implementation factors in blended synchronous learning environments: outcomes from a cross-case analysis," *Computers & Education*, vol. 86, no. 8, pp. 1–17, http://dx.doi.org/10.1016/j.compedu.2015.03.006.

Boyatzis, R 1998, *Transforming qualitative information: thematic analysis and code development*, Sage, Thousand Oaks.

Bransford, JD & Schwartz, DL 1999, Rethinking transfer: a simple proposal with multiple implications, in A Iran-Nejad and P Pearson (eds.), *Review of research in education*, American Educational Research Association AERA, Washington, D.C., pp. 61–102, viewed 24 June 2017, <http://artstart2011.pbworks.com/f/Bransford%2B%2526%2BSchwartz-transfer.pdf>.

Braun, V & Clarke, V 2006, "Using thematic analysis in psychology," *Qualitative Research in Psychology*, vol. 3, no. 2, pp. 77–101, http://dx.doi.org/10.1191/1478088706qp063oa.

_____ 2013, *Successful qualitative research: a practical guide for beginners*, Sage, Thousand Oaks, viewed 24 June 2017, <http://eprints.uwe.ac.uk/21156/3/SQR%2520Chap%25201%2520Research%2520Repository.pdf>.

Bruck, B 2007, "Speed to proficiency: strategically using training to drive profitability," viewed 24 June 2017, <http://www.q2learning.com/docs/WP-S2P.pdf>.

_____ 2015, *Speed to proficiency: creating a sustainable competitive advantage*, CreateSpace, USA, viewed 24 June 2017, <http://www.readings.com.au/products/20647385/speed-to-proficiency-creating-a-sustainable-competitive-advantage>.

Carpenter, MA, Monaco, SJ, O'Mara, FE & Teachout, MS 1989, *Time to Job Proficiency: A Preliminary Investigation of the Effects of Aptitude and Experience on Productive Capacity*, Report No. AFHRK-TP-88-17, Air Force Systems Command, Brooks Air Force Base, San Antonio, viewed 24 June 2017, <https://www.researchgate.net/publication/235105070>.

Carroll, JB 1963, "A model of school learning," *Teachers College Record*, vol. 64, pp. 723–733.

Chevalier, R 2004, "The link between learning and performance," *Performance Improvement*, vol. 43, no. 4, pp. 40–44, http://dx.doi.org/10.1002/pfi.4140430410.

Chi, MT, Glaser, R & Farr, M (eds) 1988, *The nature of expertise*, Lawrence Erlbaum, Hillsdale, http://dx.doi.org/10.4324/9781315799681.

Clark, RC 2008, *Building expertise: cognitive methods for training and performance improvement*, 3rd edn, Pfeiffer, San Francisco, http://dx.doi.org/10.1002/pfi.4140390213.

Clark, RC & Mayer, RE 2011, *E-learning and the science of instruction: proven guidelines for consumers and designers of multimedia learning*, 3rd edn, Jossey-Bass, San Francisco, http://dx.doi.org/10.1002/9781118255971.

_____ 2013, *Scenario-based e-learning: evidence-based guidelines for online workforce learning*, Pfeiffer, San Francisco.

Crichton, M & Flin, R 2004, "Identifying and training non-technical skills of nuclear emergency response teams," *Annals of Nuclear Energy*, vol. 31, no. 12, pp. 1317–1330, http://dx.doi.org/doi:10.1016/j.anucene.2004.03.011.

Darrah, CN 1996, *Learning and work: An exploration in industrial ethnography*, Routledge, New York, viewed 24 October 2018, <https://content.taylorfrancis.com/books/download?dac=C2010-0-48169-8&isbn=9781136513855&format=googlePreviewPdf>.

Davachi, L, Kiefer, T, Rock, D & Rock, L 2010, "Learning that lasts through ages," *NeuroLeadership Journal*, vol. 3, no. 3, pp. 1–13, viewed 24 June 2017, <https://www.ahri.com.au/__data/assets/pdf_file/0016/16144/Learning-that-lasts-through-AGES.pdf>.

Dean, PJ 2016, "Tom gilbert: engineering performance with or without training," *Performance Improvement*, vol. 55, no. 2, pp. 30–38, http://dx.doi.org/10.1002/pfi.21556.

DiBello, L & Missildine, W 2008, "Information technologies and intuitive expertise: a method for implementing complex organizational change among New York city transit authority's bus maintainers," *Cognition, Technology and Work*, vol. 12, no. 1, pp. 61–75, http://dx.doi.org/10.1007/s10111-008-0126-z.

_____ 2011, "Future of immersive instructional design for the global knowledge economy: a case study of an IBM project management training in virtual worlds," *International Journal of Web Based Learning and Teaching Technologies*, vol. 6, no. 3, pp. 14–34, http://dx.doi.org/10.4018/jwltt,2011070102.

_____ 2013, The future of immersive instructional design for the global knowledge economy: a case study of an IBM project, in N Karacapilidis, M Raisinghani & E Ng (eds.), *Web-Based and Blended Educational Tools and Innovations*, Information Science Reference, Hershey, pp. 115–135.

DiBello, L, Missildine, W & Struttman, M 2009, "Intuitive expertise and empowerment: the long-term impact of simulation training on changing accountabilities in a biotech firm," *Mind, Culture, and Activity*, vol. 16, no. 1, pp. 11–31, http://dx.doi.org/10.1080/10749030802363863.

Dirkx, JM 2001, "The power of feelings: emotion, imagination, and the construction of meaning in adult learning," *New Directions for Adult and Continuing Education*, vol. 2001, no. 89, pp. 63–72.

Dreyfus, HL & Dreyfus, SE 1986, *Mind over machine: the power of human intuition and expertise in the era of the computer*, The Free Press, New York, http://dx.doi.org/10.1109/mex.1987.4307079.

Dror, IE 2011, The paradox of human expertise: why experts get it wrong, in N Kapur (ed.), *The paradoxical brain*, Cambridge University Press, New York, pp. 177–188, http://dx.doi.org/10.1017/cbo9780511978098.011.

Dror, IE, Schmidt, P & O'connor, L 2011, "A cognitive perspective on technology enhanced learning in medical training: great opportunities, pitfalls and challenges," *Medical Teacher*, vol. 33, no. 4, pp. 291–6, http://dx.doi.org/10.3109/0142159X.2011.550970.

Eades, J 2014, "Why microlearning is huge and how to be a part of it," viewed 24 June 2018, <http://elearningindustry. com/why-microlearning-is-huge>.

Eraut, M 2007, *Learning in the Workplace: Research Summary for House of Commons Committee*, House of Commons Committee, London.

Ericsson, KA & Charness, N 1994, "Expert performance: its structure and acquisition," *American Psychologist*, vol. 49, no. 8, pp. 725–747, http://dx.doi.org/10.1037/0003-066X.49.8.725.

Ericsson, KA, Krampe, RTR, Tesch-romer, C, Ashworth, C, Carey, G, Grassia, J, Hastie, R, Heizmann, S, Kellogg, R, Levin, R, Lewis, C, Oliver, W, Poison, P, Rehder, R, Schlesinger, K, Schneider, V & Tesch-Römer, C 1993, "The role of deliberate practice in the acquisition of expert performance," *Psychological Review*, vol. 100, no. 3, pp. 363–406, http://dx.doi.org/10.1037/0033-295X.100.3.363.

Fadde, PJ 2007, "Instructional design for advanced learners: training recognition skills to hasten expertise," *Educational Technology Research and Development*, vol. 57, no. 3, pp. 359–376, http://dx.doi.org/10.1007/s11423-007-9046-5.

_____ 2009a, Training complex psychomotor performance skills: a part-task approach, in K Silber & W Foshay (eds.), *Handbook of Training and Improving Workplace Performance, Volume I: Instructional Design and Training Delivery*, Pfeiffer, San Francisco, pp. 468–507, http://dx.doi.org/10.1002/9780470587089.ch14.

_____ 2009b, "Training of expertise and expert performance," *Technology, Instructional, Cognition and Learning*, vol. 7, no. 2, pp. 77–81, viewed 24 June 2017, <http://web.coehs.siu.edu/Units/CI/Faculty/PFadde/Research/xbtintro.pdf>.

_____ 2009c, "Expertise-based training: getting more learners over the bar in less time," *Technology, Instructional, Cognition and Learning*, vol. 7, no. 2, pp. 171–197, viewed 24 June 2017, <http://web.coehs.siu.edu/units/ci/faculty/pfadde/Research/xbttraining.pdf>.

_____ 2010, "Look'ma, no hands: part-task training of perceptual-cognitive skills to accelerate psychomotor expertise," *The Interservice Industry Training, Simulation and Education Conference (I/ITSEC)*, Orlando, National Training and Simulation Association (NTSA), Arlington, pp. 1–10, viewed 24 June 2017, <http://ntsa.metapress.com/index/A4018183135VJ842.pdf>.

_____ 2012, "What's wrong with this picture? video-annotation with expert-model feedback as a method of accelerating novices' situation awareness," *The Interservice Industry Training, Simulation and Education Conference (I/ITSEC)*, London, National Training and Simulation Association (NTSA), Arlington, viewed 24 June 2017, <http://www.peterfadde.com/Research/iitsec12.pdf>.

_____ 2013, "Accelerating the acquisition of intuitive decision-making through expertise-based training (XBT)," *The Interservice Industry Training, Simulation and Education Conference (I/ITSEC)*, Orlando, National Training and Simulation Association (NTSA), Arlington, pp. 1–11, viewed 24 June 2017, <http://peterfadde.com/Research/iitsec13.pdf>.

_____ 2016, "Instructional design for accelerated macrocognitive expertise in the baseball workplace," *Frontiers in Psychology*, vol. 7, no. 292, pp. 1–16, http://dx.doi.org/10.3389/fpsyg.2016.00292.

Fadde, PJ & Klein, G 2010, "Deliberate performance: accelerating expertise in natural settings," *Performance Improvement*, vol. 49, no. 9, pp. 5–14, http://dx.doi.org/10.1002/pfi.

_____ 2012, "Accelerating expertise using action learning activities," *Cognitive Technology*, vol. 17, no. 1, pp. 11–18, viewed 24 June 2017, <http://peterfadde.com/Research/cognitivetechnology12.pdf>.

Fred, CL 2002, *Breakaway: deliver value to your customers-fast!*, Jossey-Bass, San Francisco, viewed 24 June 2017, <http://www.wiley.com/WileyCDA/WileyTitle/productCd-0787961647.html>.

Gallagher, AG, Ritter, EM, Champion, H, Higgins, G, Fried, MP, Moses, G, Smith, CD & Satava, RM 2005, "Virtual reality simulation for the operating room: proficiency-based training as a paradigm shift in surgical skills training.," *Annals of Surgery*, vol. 241, no. 2, pp. 364–72.

Gery, GJ 1991, *Electronic performance support systems: how and why to remake the workplace through the strategic application of technology*, Weingarten, Bostom.

Gordon, TJ 1994, The Delphi method, in J Glenn & T Gordon (eds.), *Futures research methodology - Version 3.0*, The Millennium Project, Washington, D.C., viewed 24 June 2017, <http://millennium-project.org/FRMv3_0/04-Delphi.pdf>.

Gott, SP & Lesgold, AM 2000, Competence in the workplace: how cognitive performance models and situated instruction can accelerate skill acquisition, in R Glaser (ed.), *Advances in instructional psychology: Educational design and cognitive science, Vol. 5*, Lawrence Erlbaum, Mahwah, pp. 239–327.

Government Publishing Office 2013, *Pilot Certification and Qualification Requirements for Air Carrier*, No. 78, Government Publishing Office, USA.

Grossman, R, Salas, E, Pavlas, D & Rosen, MA 2013, "Using instructional features to enhance demonstration-based training in management education," *Academy of Management Learning & Education*, vol. 12, no. 2, pp. 219–243, http://dx.doi.org/10.5465/amle.2011.0527.

Grovo 2014, "Bite size is the right size: how microlearning shrinks the skills gap," *TechKnowledge 2015*, p. 2105, viewed 24 June 2017, <http://a1.grovo.com/asset/whitepapers/Grovo-BiteSize-Microlearning-whitepaper.pdf>.

Guskey, T 2009, "Mastery learning," viewed 24 June 2017, <http://www.education.com/reference/article/mastery-learning/>.

Higgins, N 2015, *Gamification: Accelerating Learning*, KBR Kellogg Brown and Root Pty Ltd, Kingston, ACT, Australia.

Hinterberger, H 2011, "Problem-based e-learning in practice: digital laboratories provide pathways from e-science to high schools," in C Ho and M Lin (eds.), *Proceedings of World Conference on E-Learning in Corporate, Government, Healthcare, and Higher Education*, 18 October, Association for the Advancement of Computing in Education (AACE), Chesapeake, pp. 1947–1954, viewed 24 June 2017, < http://www.editlib.org/p/39013/>.

Hintze, NR 2008, "First responder problem solving and decision making in today's asymmetrical environment," Naval Postgraduate School, Monterey, viewed 24 June 2017, <http://www.dtic.mil/cgi-bin/GetTRDoc?AD=ADA479926>.

Hoffman, R, Feltovich, PJ, Fiore, S, Klein, G & Moon, B 2008, *Program on Technology Innovation: Accelerating the Achievement of Mission-Critical Expertise: A Research Roadmap*, Report No. 1016710, Electric Power Research Institute (EPRI), Palo Alto, viewed 24 June 2017, <http://perigeantechnologies.com/publications/AcceleratingAchievementofExpertise.pdf>.

Hoffman, RR & Andrews, DH 2012, "Cognition and cognitive technology for research on accelerated learning and developing expertise," *Cognitive Technology*, vol. 17, no. 1, pp. 5–6, viewed 24 June 2017, <http://cmapsinternal.ihmc.us/rid=1LM7CN14D-1335H6-1B3K/CogTech%20for%20Accelerated%20Learning-2013.pdf>.

Hoffman, RR, Andrews, DH & Feltovich, PJ 2012, "What is 'accelerated learning'?," *Cognitive Technology*, vol. 17, no. 1, pp. 7–10.

Hoffman, RR, Andrews, DH, Fiore, SM, Goldberg, S, Andre, T, Freeman, J, Fletcher, JD & Klein, G 2010, "Accelerated learning: prospects, issues and applications," *Proceedings of the Human Factors and Ergonomics Society 54th Annual Meeting*, San Francisco, 27 September - 1 October, Sage, Thousand Oaks, pp. 399–402, http://dx.doi.org/10.1177/154193121005400427.

Hoffman, RR, Feltovich, PJ, Fiore, SM & Klein, G 2010, *Accelerated Proficiency and Facilitated Retention: Recommendations Based on an Integration of Research and Findings from a Working Meeting*, Report No. AFRL-RH-AZ-TR-2011-0001, Air Force Research Laboratory, Mesa, http://dx.doi.org/10.21236/ada536308.

Hoffman, RR, Feltovich, PJ, Fiore, SM, Klein, G & Ziebell, D 2009, "Accelerated learning (?)," *IEEE Intelligent Systems*, vol. 24, no. 2, pp. 18–22, http://dx.doi.org/10.1109/MIS.2009.21.

Hoffman, RR, Ward, P, Feltovich, PJ, DiBello, L, Fiore, SM & Andrews, DH 2014, *Accelerated Expertise: Training for high proficiency in a complex world*, Expertise: Research and Applications Series, Psychology Press, New York, http://dx.doi.org/10.4324/9780203797327.

Hug, T 2015, Microlearning and mobile learning, in Z Yan (ed.), *Encyclopedia of Mobile Phone Behavior*, IGI Global, Hersey, pp. 490–505, http://dx.doi.org/10.4018/978-1-4666-8239-9.ch041.

Hug, T, Lindner, M & Bruck, PA (eds) 2006, *Micromedia & E-Learning 2.0: Gaining the Big Picture: Proceedings of Microlearning Conference 2006*, Innsbruck, 25-27 June, Innsbruck University Press, Innsbruck, Austria, viewed 24 June 2017, <https://www.uibk.ac.at/iup/buch_pdfs/microlearning2006-druck.pdf>.

Hughes, BD 2003, "Performance-based instruction: training that works," , no. August, pp. 1–38.

Hutchins, E & Palen, L 1997, Constructing meaning from space, gesture, and speech, in *Discourse, tools and reasoning*, Springer, Berlin, pp. 23–40, viewed 24 October 2018, <http://citeseerx.ist.psu.edu/viewdoc/download?doi=10.1.1.161.1357&rep=rep1&type=pdf>.

Imel, S 2002, "Accelerated learning in adult education and training and development," *Trends and Issue Alerts No. 33*, pp. 1–2, viewed 24 June 2017, <http://www.calpro-online.org/ERIC/docs/tia00101.pdf>.

Jacobs, R & Hawley, J 2002, Emergence of workforce development: definition, conceptual boundaries, and future perspectives, in R MacLean & D Wilson (eds.), *International Handbook of Technical and Vocational Education and Training*, Kluwer, Amsterdam, viewed 24 June 2018, <http://www.economicmodeling.com/wp-content/uploads/2007/11/jacobs_hawley-emergenceofworkforcedevelopment.pdf>.

Jacobs, RL 2003, *Structured on-the-job training: Unleashing employee expertise in the workplace*, 2nd edn, Berrett-Koehler, San Francisco.

_____ 2014, Structured on-the-job training, in R Poell, T Rocco & G Roth (eds.), *The Routledge Companion to Human Resource Development*, Routledge, Oxon, pp. 272–284.

Jacobs, RL & Bu-Rahmah, MJ 2012, "Developing employee expertise through structured on-the-job training (s-ojt): an introduction to this training approach and the KNPC experience," *Industrial and Commercial Training*, vol. 44, no. 2, pp. 75–84, http://dx.doi.org/10.1108/00197851211202902.

Jenkins, JT, Currie, A, Sala, S & Kennedy, RH 2016, "A multi-modal approach to training in laparoscopic colorectal surgery accelerates proficiency gain," *Surgical Endoscopy*, vol. 30, no. 7, pp. 3007–3013, http://dx.doi.org/10.1007/s00464-015-4591-1.

Jennings, C & Wargnier, J 2010, "Experiential learning-a way to develop agile minds in the knowledge economy?," *Development and Learning in Organizations*, vol. 24, no. 3, pp. 14–16, http://dx.doi.org/10.1108/14777281011037245.

Jonassen, DH & Hung, W 2008, "All problems are not equal: implications for problem-based learning," *Interdisciplinary Journal of Problem Solving*, vol. 2, no. 2, pp. 10–13, http://dx.doi.org/10.7771/1541-5015.1080.

De Jonge, M, Tabbers, HK, Pecher, D, Jang, Y & Zeelenberg, R 2015, "The efficacy of self-paced study in multitrial learning," *JOurnal of Experimental Psychology, Learning, Memory, and Cognition*, vol. 41, no. 3, pp. 851–858, http://dx.doi.org/10.1037/xlm0000046.

Kahiigi Kigozi, E, Ekenberg, L, Hansson, H, Tusubira, F & Danielson, M 2008, "Exploring the e-learning state of art," *Electronic Journal of E-Learning*, vol. 6, no. 2, pp. 77–88, viewed <http://www.diva-portal.org/smash/record.jsf?pid=diva2:185115>.

Kang, S "Pil" 2017, "What do hpt consultants do for performance analysis?," *TechTrends*, vol. 61, no. 1, pp. 32–45, http://dx.doi.org/10.1007/s11528-016-0129-1.

Karoly, LA & Panis, CW 2004, *The 21st century at work: forces shaping the future workforce and workplace in the United States*, Rand Corporation, Santa Monica, http://dx.doi.org/10.1037/e527212012-001.

Karpicke, JD & Bauernschmidt, A 2011, "Spaced retrieval: absolute spacing enhances learning regardless of relative spacing," *Journal of Experimental Psychology, Learning, Memory, and Cognition*, vol. 37, no. 5, pp. 1250–1257, http://dx.doi.org/10.1037/a0023436.

Klein, GA 2003, *Intuition at work: why developing your gut instinct will make you better at what you do,*, Currency Doubleday, New York.

Klein, GA & Borders, J 2016, "The shadowbox approach to cognitive skills training an empirical evaluation," *Journal of Cognitive Engineering and Decision Making*, vol. 10, no. 3, pp. 268–280, http://dx.doi.org/10.1177/1555343416636515.

Klein, GA, Hintze, N & Saab, D 2013, "Thinking inside the box: the shadowbox method for cognitive skill development," in H Chaudet, L Pellegrin & N Bonnardel (eds.), *Proceedings of the 11th International Conference on Naturalistic Decision Making*, Marseille, 21-24 May, Aepege Science Publishing, Paris, pp. 121–124, viewed 24 June 2017, <http://arpege-recherche.org/ndm11/papers/ndm11-121.pdf>.

Kolozsvari, NO, Kaneva, P, Brace, C, Chartrand, G, Vaillancourt, M, Cao, J, Banaszek, D, Demyttenaere, S, Vassiliou, MC, Fried, GM & Feldman, LS 2011, "Mastery versus the standard proficiency target for basic laparoscopic skill training: effect on skill transfer and retention.," *Surgical Endoscopy*, vol. 25, no. 7, pp. 2063–70, http://dx.doi.org/10.1007/s00464-011-1743-9.

Kort, B, Reilly, R & Picard, RW 2001, "An affective model of interplay between emotions and learning: reengineering educational pedagogy-building a learning companion," *Proceeding of IEEE International Conference on Advanced Learning Technologies, 2001*, IEEE Computer Society Press, Los Alamitos, pp. 43–46, viewed 24 January 2019, <https://www.researchgate.net/profile/Barry_Kort/publication/228975170>.

Kraiger, K 2014, "Looking back and looking forward: trends in training and development research," *Human Resource Development Quarterly*, vol. 25, no. 4, pp. 401–408, http://dx.doi.org/10.1002/hrdq.21203.

Kuchenbrod, R 2016, "Accelerating expertise to facilitate decision making in high-risk professions using the DOCUM system," PhD thesis, Eastern Illinois University, Charleston, viewed 24 June 2017, <http://thekeep.eiu.edu/cgi/viewcontent.cgi?article=3462&context=theses>.

Lajoie, SP 2003, "Transitions and trajectories for studies of expertise," *Educational Researcher*, vol. 32, no. 8, pp. 21–25, http://dx.doi.org/10.3102/0013189X032008021.

Lee, PWY 2011, "Structured proficiency based progression phacoemulsification training curriculum using virtual reality simulator technology," Master's thesis, Royal College of Surgeons in Ireland, Dublin, Ireland, viewed 24 June 2017, <http://epubs.rcsi.ie/cgi/viewcontent.cgi?article=1007&context=mchrestheses.

Lesgold, AM 1991, *Methodological Foundations for Designing Intelligent Computer-Based Training*, Research Report No. N00014-89-J-1168, Office of Naval Research, Arlington, viewed 24 June 2017, <http://www.dtic.mil/dtic/tr/fulltext/u2/a257925.pdf>.

Lesgold, AM, Lajoie, S, Bunzo, M & Eggan, G 1988, *Sherlock: A Coached Practice Environment for an Electronics Troubleshooting Job*, Report No. AD-A201-748, University of Pittsburg, Pittsburg, PA, viewed 24 June 2017, <http://eric.ed.gov/?id=ED299450>.

Lincoln, YS & Guba, EG 1985, *Naturalistic inquiry*, Sage, Newbury Park.

Lingg, D 2014, "Bite-size learning marks the road to workforce efficiency," *MHD Supply Chain Solutions*, vol. 44, no. 5, pp. 1–12, viewed 24 June 2017, <http://search.informit.com.au/documentSummary;dn=740763588509945;res=IELENG>.

Marker, A, Villachica, SW, Stepich, D, Allen, D & Stanton, L 2014, "An updated framework for human performance improvement in the workplace: the spiral HPI framework," *Performance Improvement*, vol. 53, no. 1, pp. 10–23, http://dx.doi.org/10.1002/pfi.21389.

Mason, J 2002, *Qualitative researching*, 2nd edn, Sage, Thousand Oaks.

Mayer, RE & Moreno, R 2003, "Nine ways to reduce cognitive load in multimedia learning," *Educational Psychologist*, vol. 38, no. 1, pp. 43–52, http://dx.doi.org/10.1207/S15326985EP3801_6.

Van der Meer, J, Berg, D, Smith, J, Gunn, A & Anakin, M 2015, "Shorter is better: findings of a bite-size mobile learning (tm) pilot project," *Creative Education*, vol. 6, no. 3, pp. 273–282, http://dx.doi.org/10.4236/ce.2015.63026.

Merriam, SB & Tisdell, EJ 2016, *Qualitative research: a guide to design and implementation*, 4th edn, Jossey-Bass, San Francisco.

Van Merriënboer, JJG, Clark, RE & de Croock, MBM 2002, "Blueprints for complex learning: the 4c/id-model," *Educational Technology Research and Development*, vol. 50, no. 2, pp. 39–61, http://dx.doi.org/10.1007/BF02504993.

Miles, MB & Huberman, AM 1994, *Qualitative data analysis: An expanded sourcebook*, 2nd edn, Sage, Thousand Oaks.

Miles, MB, Huberman, AM & Saldana, J 2014, *Qualitative data analysis: a methods sourcebook*, 3rd edn, Sage, Thousand Oaks.

Millington, R 2018, 10.10: measuring time-to-full productivity, in *How to Calculate the ROI of online Communities*, FeverBee Ltd, London, viewed 24 October 2018, <https://www.feverbee.com/roi/measuring-time-to-full-productivity/>.

Nagel, D 2011, "Beyond seat time: advancing proficiency-based learning," *The Journal: Transforming Education*, viewed 24 June 2017, <https://thejournal.com/articles/2011/08/10/beyond-seat-time-advancing-proficiency-based-learning.aspx>.

Nguyen, F 2006, "What you already know does matter: expertise and electronic performance support systems," *Performance Improvement*, vol. 45, no. 4, pp. 9–12, http://dx.doi.org/10.1002/pfi.2006.4930450404.

Pappas, C 2013, "Top 10 e-learning statistics for 2014 you need to know," viewed 24 June 2017, <http://elearningindustry.com/top-10-e-learning-statistics-for-2014-you-need-to-know>.

Patchan, MM, Schunn, CD, Sieg, W & McLaughlin, D 2015, "The effect of blended instruction on accelerated learning," *Technology, Pedagogy and Education*, vol. 25, no. 3, pp. 1–18, http://dx.doi.org/10.1080/1475939X.2015.1013977.

Pershing, JA (ed) 2006, *Handbook of human performance technology: principles, practices, and potential*, 3rd edn, Pfeiffer, San Francisco.

Phillips, JK, Klein, G & Sieck, WR 2004, Expertise in judgment and decision making: a case for training intuitive decision skills, in D Koehler and N Harvey (eds.), *Blackwell handbook of judgment and decision making*, Blackwell, Malden, pp. 297–315, http://dx.doi.org/10.1002/9780470752937.ch15.

Pinder, CC & Schroeder, KG 1987, "Time to proficiency following job transfers," *Academy of Management Journal*, vol. 30, no. 2, pp. 336–353, http://dx.doi.org/10.2307/256278.

Pollock, RV, Wick, CW & Jefferson, A 2015, *The six disciplines of breakthrough learning: how to turn training and development into business results*, 3rd edn, John Wiley, San Francisco.

Radler, D & Bocianu, I 2017, "Accelerated teaching and learning: roles and challenges for learners and tutors," *The International Scientific Conference eLearning and Software for Education*, Bucharest, ProQuest, Ann Arbor, pp. 601–608, http://dx.doi.org/10.12753/2066-026X-17-170.

Raybould, B 1995, "Performance support engineering: an emerging development methodology for enabling organizational learning," *Performance Improvement*

*Quarterly*, vol. 8, no. 1, pp. 7–22, http://dx.doi.org/10.1111/j.1937-8327.1995.tb00658.x.

Rosenbaum, S & Pollock, R 2015, "Creating a conducive talent development and learning culture," paper presented to the ATD International Conference and Exposition, Orlando.

Rosenbaum, S & Williams, J 2004, *Learning paths: increase profits by reducing the time it takes employees to get up to speed*, Jossey-Bass, San Francisco, viewed 24 June 2017, <http://www.wiley.com/WileyCDA/WileyTitle/productCd-0787975346.html>.

Rosenberg, MJ 2001, *E-Learning: Strategies for Delivering Knowledge in the Digital Age*, McGraw-Hill, New York.

Rosenthal, ME, Castellvi, AO, Goova, MT, Hollett, LA, Dale, J & Scott, DJ 2009, "Pretraining on southwestern stations decreases training time and cost for proficiency-based fundamentals of laparoscopic surgery training," *Journal of the American College of Surgeons*, vol. 209, no. 5, pp. 626–631, http://dx.doi.org/10.1016/j.jamcollsurg.2009.07.013.

Rothwell, WJ & Kazanas, HC 2004, *Improving on-the-job training: How to establish and operate a comprehensive OJT program*, John Wiley & Sons, San Francisco.

Saks, A, Haccoun, R & Belcourt, M 2010, *Managing performance through training and development*, 5th edn, Nelson Education, Canada, viewed 24 June 2017, <https://www.amazon.com/Managing-Performance-Through-Training-Development/dp/0176507337>.

Salas, E, Tannenbaum, SI, Kraiger, K & Smith-Jentsch, K a 2012, "The science of training and development in organizations: what matters in practice," *Psychological Science in the Public Interest*, vol. 13, no. 2, pp. 74–101, http://dx.doi.org/10.1177/1529100612436661.

Schuwirth, L 2013, "'emotions in learning' is more than merely 'learning of emotions,'" *Medical Education*, vol. 47, no. 1, pp. 3–17, http://dx.doi.org/10.1111/medu.12078.

Scott, DJ, Ritter, EM, Tesfay, ST, Pimentel, EA, Nagji, A & Fried, GM 2008, "Certification pass rate of 100% for fundamentals of laparoscopic surgery skills after proficiency-based training.," *Surgical Endoscopy*, vol. 22, no. 8, pp. 1887–93, http://dx.doi.org/10.1007/s00464-008-9745-y.

Sheckley, B & Keeton, M 1999, *Ecologies that support and enhance adult learning*, College Park: University of Maryland College.

Shen, L, Wang, M & Shen, R 2009, "Affective e-learning: using 'emotional' data to improve learning in pervasive learning environment related work and the pervasive e-learning platform," *Educational Technology & Society*, vol. 12, no. 2, pp. 176–189, viewed 24 June 2017, <http://www.ifets.info/journals/12_2/13.pdf>.

Sims, DE, Burke, CS, Metcalf, DS & Salas, E 2008, "Research-based guidelines for designing blended learning," *Ergonomics in Design: The Quarterly of Human Factors Applications*, vol. 16, no. 1, pp. 23–29, http://dx.doi.org/10.1518/106480408X282764.

Sitzmann, T 2010, "Game on? the effectiveness of game use in the workplace depends on context and design," *T+D*, vol. 20, p. 20, viewed 24 June 2017, <https://www.moresteam.com/whitepapers/download/sitzmann-games2010.pdf>.

Slootmaker, A, Kurvers, H, Hummel, H & Koper, R 2014, "Developing scenario-based serious games for complex cognitive skills acquisition: design, development and evaluation of the emergo platform," *Journal of Universal Computer Science*, vol. 20, no. 4, pp. 561–582, http://dx.doi.org/10.3217/jucs-020-04-0561.

Soderstrom, NC & Bjork, RA 2015, "Learning versus performance: an integrative review," *Perspectives on Psychological Science*, vol. 10, no. 2, pp. 176–199, http://dx.doi.org/10.1177/1745691615569000.

Stake, RE 2006, *Multiple case study analysis*, The Guilford Press, New York, viewed 24 June 2017, <http://www.guilford.com/books/Multiple-Case-Study-Analysis/Robert-Stake/9781593852481>.

Stefanidis, D, Korndorffer, JR, Markley, S, Sierra, R & Scott, DJ 2006, "Proficiency maintenance: impact of ongoing simulator training on laparoscopic skill retention," *Journal of the American College of Surgeons*, vol. 202, no. 4, pp. 599–603, http://dx.doi.org/10.1016/j.jamcollsurg.2005.12.018.

Sternberg, RJ 1999, "Intelligence as developing expertise.," *Contemporary Educational Psychology*, vol. 24, no. 4, pp. 359–375, http://dx.doi.org/10.1006/ceps.1998.0998.

Stewart, J & Dohme, JA 2005, "Automated hover trainer: simulator-based intelligent flight training system," *International Journal of Applied Aviation Studies*, vol. 5, no. 1, pp. 25–40, viewed 24 October 2018, <https://pdfs.semanticscholar.org/b959/00872b74560e59c33864e1a7642aafbbe23c.pdf#page=25>.

Stolovitch, HD 2000, "Human performance technology: research and theory to practice," *Performance Improvement*, vol. 39, no. 4, pp. 7–16, http://dx.doi.org/10.1002/pfi.4140390407.

Swanson, RA & Holton III, EF 2001, *Foundations of human resource development*, Berrett-Koehler, Oakland, viewed 24 June 2017, <https://www.bkconnection.com/static/Foundations_of_Human_Resource_De

velopment_EXCERPT.pdf>.

Thalheimer, W 2006, *Spacing Learning over Time*, Work-Learning Research, Somerville.

Thompson, KS 2017, Training's impact on time-to-proficiency for new bankers in a financial services organization, in S Frasard & P Frederick (eds.), *Training Initiatives and Strategies for the Modern Workforce*, IGI Global, Hershey, pp. 169–185, http://dx.doi.org/10.4018/978-1-5225-1808-2.ch009.

Van Tiem, D, Moseley, JL & Dessinger, JC 2012, *Fundamentals of performance improvement: optimizing results through people, process, and organizations*, 3rd edn, Pfeiffer, San Francisco.

Trekles, AM & Sims, R 2013, "Designing instruction for speed: qualitative insights into instructional design for accelerated online graduate coursework," *Online Journal of Distance Learning Administration*, vol. 16, no. 3, viewed 24 June 2017, <http://www.westga.edu/~distance/ojdla/winter164/trekles_sims164.html>.

Trigwell, K, Ellis, R a & Han, F 2012, "Relations between students' approaches to learning, experienced emotions and outcomes of learning," *Studies in Higher Education*, vol. 37, no. 7, pp. 811–824, http://dx.doi.org/10.1080/03075079.2010.549220.

Tullis, JG & Benjamin, AS 2011, "On the effectiveness of self-paced learning," *Journal of Memory and Language*, vol. 64, no. 2, pp. 109–118, http://dx.doi.org/10.1016/j.jml.2010.11.002.

Turner, JR & Müller, R 2003, "On the nature of the project as a temporary organization," *International Journal of Project Management*, vol. 21, no. 1, pp. 1–8, http://dx.doi.org/10.1016/s0263-7863(02)00020-0.

Värlander, S 2008, "The role of students' emotions in formal feedback situations," *Teaching in Higher Education*, vol. 13, no. 2, pp. 145–156, http://dx.doi.org/10.1080/13562510801923195.

Vaughan, K 2008, *Workplace Learning: A Literature Review*, The New Zealand Engineering Food & Manufacturing Industry Training Organisation Incorporated, Auckland, viewed 24 June 2017, <https://www.akoaotearoa.ac.nz/download/ng/file/group-189/n1575-workplace-learning-a-literature-review.pdf>.

Vohra, V 2014, "Using the multiple case study design to decipher contextual leadership behaviors in Indian organizations," *Electronic Journal of Business Research Methods*, vol. 12, no. 1, pp. 54–65, viewed 24 June 2017, <http://www.ejbrm.com/issue/download.html?idArticle=334>.

Wallace, GW 2006, Modeling mastery performance and systematically deriving the enablers for performance improvement, in J Pershing (ed.), *Handbook of human performance technology: Principles, practices, and potential*, Pfeiffer, San Francisco, viewed 24 June 2017,

<http://widyo.staff.gunadarma.ac.id/Downloads/files/20372/HANDBOOK+OF+HPT_THIRD+EDITION.pdf#page=284>.

Wilcox, V, Trus, T, Salas, N, Martinez, J & Dunkin, BJ 2014, "A proficiency-based skills training curriculum for the sages surgical training for endoscopic proficiency (step) program," *Journal of Surgical Education*, vol. 71, no. 3, pp. 282–288, http://dx.doi.org/10.1016/j.jsurg.2013.10.004.

Wray, A & Wallace, M 2011, "Accelerating the development of expertise: a step-change in social science research capacity building," *British Journal of Educational Studies*, vol. 59, no. 3, pp. 241–264, http://dx.doi.org/10.1080/00071005.2011.599790.

Wulf, G & Shea, CH 2002, "Principles derived from the study of simple skills do not generalize to complex skill learning," *Psychonomic Bulletin & Review*, vol. 9, no. 2, pp. 185–211, http://dx.doi.org/10.3758/BF03196276.

Yin, RK 2014, *Case study research: design and methods*, 5th edn, Sage, Thousand Oaks.

Zhang, D 2005, "Interactive multimedia-based e-learning: a study of effectiveness," *The American Journal of Distance Education*, vol. 19, no. 3, pp. 149–162, http://dx.doi.org/10.1207/s15389286ajde1903_3
.

'

# INDEX

## Speed To Proficiency
### RESEARCH

*Accelerated Performance for Accelerated Times*

**Highly-specialized know-how, learning, and resources to solve challenges of 'time' and 'speed' in performance at organizational, professional and personal levels.**

Visit us at https://www.speedtoproficiency.com/

**S2Pro© Speed To Proficiency Research** is a corporate research and consulting forum that provides authentic guidelines to business practitioners to accelerate proficiency of their workforce, teams, and professionals at the 'speed of business'. S2Pro© publishes reports, ebooks, and articles exclusively related to accelerated performance, accelerated proficiency and accelerated expertise in the individual and organizational context. Our extensive knowledge base of "how to methods" is derived from experience-based and practice-based observations, analysis/synthesis of existing research, or based on planned/focused research studies through a network of researchers who exclusively focus on 'time' and 'speed' metrics in the business context.

Speed To Proficiency Research: S2Pro©
*A research and consulting forum*
Singapore

Website: https://www.speedtoproficiency.com
e-mail: rkattri@speedtoproficiency.com
Facebook: https://www.facebook.com/speedtoproficiency/
LinkedIn: https://www.linkedin.com/company/speedtoproficiency/
Twitter: https://www.twitter.com/speed2expertise
Google+: https://plus.google.com/101561704929830160312

Printed in Great
Britain
by Amazon